REVISED EDITION

TAPESTRIES IN SAND

THE SPIRIT OF INDIAN SANDPAINTING

Paintings

DAVID

Photography by Los Angeles County Museum

Prefaced by Vinson Brown

To The Fairchilds from Nancy

Dedicated to:

Mother Earth and All Her Children
and
To My Many Indian Brothers for the

Inspiration of Their Friendship

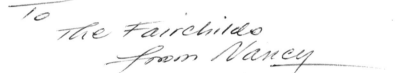

May you always walk with Beauty beside you, and with Beauty all around you

NATUREGRAPH PRESS

Published by Naturegraph Company, Healdsburg, California

2

*** TABLE OF CONTENTS ***

PREFACE - ABOUT THE AUTHOR

By Vinson Brown

When I first met David V. Villaseñor in February, 1963 at the Great Council Fire of thirty Indian tribes at Camp Palos Verdes near Tucson, Arizona, I felt an instant warmth and friendship for this intensely alive and warm-hearted man. His dark eyes, set in a mahogany-tinted face, literally flashed curiosity and interest. Since then our acquaintance has grown into a deep friendship and I am very happy to be able to help with the publication of this book which I feel is written from the very depths of his heart and soul.

David was reared and educated in an Industrial and Graphic Arts School (Boys' Town), called "Cruz Galvez, " in Hermosillo, Sonora, Mexico, where nearly all of the students were of Indian descent. He himself is part Otomi Indian and has become most intimately associated with this part of his ancestory. When sick, he has been successfully treated by Otomi, Mayo, Yaqui, Papago, and Apache Medicine Men and Women (parents or relatives of his Indian school chums). On several occasions he has been the patient when sandpainting ceremonials were exclusively performed for him by his Navajo friends. At other times, by request, he has assisted in the making of the sandpaintings among the Navajos as well as at California Indian Ceremonials. In short his book is not only a biography of his life, but an esoteric interpretation of his experience in living among and being raised directly in several different Indian families.

David entered the United States when he was sixteen, and it was at this time that he saw his first sandpainting being made by a wise old Medicine Man on the Navajo Reservation for sacred ceremonial purposes. His imagination fired, he vowed then that some day he would find a means of preserving the beauty and meaning of this ancient art, which is always done loosely upon the ground and the sandpainting destroyed within a twelve hour period.

Since then he has become an expert artist and sculptor, working in this field for the Medical Corps of the U. S. Army, during which time he won high honors for his work. While in the Army he lectured at Denver and New Mexico Universities, and has continued a successful lecture career since then, concentrating more on an explanation and exposition of Indian sandpainting. His own sandpaintings have had one-man shows since 1951-52 at the Legion of Honor in San Francisco, the Southwest Museum in Highland Park, the American Museum of Natural History in New York, the Los Angeles County Museum, and many others.

PREFACE BY THE AUTHOR

In the far away days of many an Indian tribe, the picturesque costume of color and design was a symbolic record of its owner. Without a word, in the meeting of two Indians, each could read from toe to headdress a lifetime history of the other. Identified in leather, beads, stone, or feather for all to see, was his name and tribe, inclination and tradition, failure and accomplishment. "There is nothing to hide from man," says the Indian, "for does not the Great Spirit already know even that which is in our hearts?"

Each tribe still has its own identifying manner of dress, usually worn in completion now only for ceremonial purposes. So have the armed forces of the world had such identification for centuries, where anyone at a glance could identify branch and field of service, rank, and accomplishments, through color, cut, stripe, insignia and medals. Here, too, full regalia is usually worn only for ceremonial purposes.

The Indian awarded everyone in the tribe. Children and women alike could claim coups (honors) for feats of unusual daring, with these honors included in their dress. Honors were bestowed for a basket, or pottery of unusual design or beauty. Blankets, beadwork or any of their arts and crafts were, and still are, considered in many instances a prayer made visual - the song of the heart, in rhythm with dancing fingers, fashioning a work of beauty, bearing mute testimony to the inspiration of the divine urge within.

Art was a necessity among the North American Indians, as there was no written language; pictographs and symbols were widely used. Gayly decorated baskets, pottery, jewelry and all other paraphernalia had not only vital information, but also a soul quality, the reflection of the individual artist or craftsman, depicting the family, the tribe, and all of creation.

The Indian knows that the Great Spirit is not bred into man alone, but the whole of the Universe shares in the immortal perfection. The wealth of wisdom embodied in the ancient art and sacred ritual of Indian Sandpainting will equal the very best in modern psychology. And yet it is so little known and understood. It is hoped that this book, in some small way, will share with you a new appreciation of our rich American heritage.

INTRODUCTION TO SANDPAINTING

(See picture of "the Sandpainter" on page 33)

Sandpainting is a very old Southwest Indian Art in which the Medicine Man "paints" loosely upon the ground, or, on some occasions, upon buckskin or cloth, by letting the sands flow with control and skill through his sensitized fingers. He may use also, in conjunction with the sands of natural color, corn meal, flower pollen, powdered roots and bark, in the execution of this ritual.

The Medicine Man is an "Initiate" among his people, for his position has been earned not only through inclination, but after long years of apprenticeship, and through the knowledge and wisdom which comes from the harmony and contact of living close to the Source-of-All-Life, thereby qualifying him to act as the intermediary at the altar of the sacred ritual of a ceremonial sandpainting. Because of the sacred nature of this ceremony, the sandpaintings are begun, finished, used, and destroyed within a twelve hour period, and are therefore virtually unknown except in the Southwest and in those few Museums fortunate enough to have one on an immovable table under heavy plate glass.

Those who are familiar with the art of Indian Sandpainting know that its last great stronghold lies in the vastness, beauty, and wastes of the Monument Valley region. Here, so far as is known, dwell the masters of the medium, both past and present. This is the land of the rainbow colors; this is the land of Dineh-the-people, our copper-skinned brothers, the Navajo Indians.

Whether the medium is sand for painting, grasses for basket making, stones for jewelry, clay for pottery, or wool for blankets, throughout each is the same spirit of creation. And in each, the Indian of the various tribes has employed that material which is most abundant in his own locality. It is for this reason that the Navajo, native of the colored sands, has perfected this art by which to express himself, although sandpainting is done also by the Zuni and Hopi Indians, who are neighbors of the Navajos, and from whom, it is said, the Navajos were originally introduced to sandpainting. Apaches, Papagos and Southern California Indians also have done ceremonial sandpaintings in the past.

Every religion has its Holy Book and the American Indian has his spiritual heritage in a mingling of history, mythology, prophecy and symbolism which has been sacredly preserved and perpetuated with the aid of chant, ritual and design, embellished with a wonderful poetic imagination. The Great Spirit fashioned man as the elder brother of creation, the Indian believes, and the elder brother's responsibility for this endowment is to share with, and care for his "little brothers" of the animal, vegetable and mineral kingdoms. With this awareness, the Medicine Man traces upon the sands those traditions of the living spirit embodying the Great Mystery of Life, wherein every color and line forms a precious seed of ancient wisdom which has been carried down through the ages for him who can understand to resurrect into a quickening force.

The ritual of sandpainting is ordinarily done in a sequence which is termed a "chant", lasting from five to nine days, but never less than three days, and for which a different sandpainting is made anew each day. Long prayers, intoned like a litany consisting of a series of invocations, suggest the term "chant". Many other rituals, exacting in detail and traditional sequence, are included to attract the "Spirit People", who usually attend and often assist in this sacred ceremony. It is often said that if the rituals are performed correctly, the prayer sticks placed properly, the chants sung beautifully, and the sandpainting done masterfully, the spirits are "compelled" to attend this ceremony held in their honor. [9]

The Medicine Man first goes through a three day period of purification, fasting, sweating and emesis, sexual restraint, bathing, and a lone vigil, for he knows that these disciplines bring him in touch with a magnetic and static force that concentrates in solitude. This is the dynamic force that will use him to heal, to bless the patient, to instruct, restore and make whole again. It is an exacting knowledge that he must use, and one that is not acquired quickly.

During this three day period of purification the Medicine Man is also collecting his sands, flower pollen, ground cornmeal, roots and barks that will be used for the sacred sandpainting. Each of these steps is done with the utmost reverence, recognizing the privilege and the occasion of worshiping the Great Spirit by rendering service to his fellowman. To share the fruits of his skill and success is an accepted way of life among the American Indians.

There are two definite types of sandpaintings, those that belong to the rhythm of the night and those that belong to the rhythm of the day. Nature behaves differently during the night, so man, like his brothers of the animal and the vegetable kingdoms, must do likewise. A sandpainting belonging to the night chant (see page 45) must be begun right after sunset and be made, used and destroyed before sunrise the following morning. A day sandpainting is begun at sunrise and finished, used and destroyed before sunset of the same day. When the sandpainting is finished by the Medicine Man and his assistant (sometimes there are two, three, or more assistants that work under the watchful eye of the wise one) the patient is "sung over", and, symbolically, the sandpainting is transferred from the ground onto the body of the patient, who by now is sitting right in the center of the painting, thus becoming the very essence of divine attention, the very altar of creation.

The chanting and rituals have a miraculous effect upon the patient, for the Indian knows that the healing power of the "sing" is good for a sick mind and a sad heart. The ceremony may or may not cure his physical body, but, nevertheless, he believes deeply in the power of the Ancient One that comes to help him resolve his inner conflicts by establishing a peaceful and harmonious condition within himself and the world around him. After the patient is "sung over" the sandpainting is physically transferred onto his body. The chanter dips his fingers into a liquid and then onto the sandpainting. The sand which adheres is carried over to that part of the patient's body which symbolically corresponds or harmonizes with the spirit of the sandpainting.

At the ceremony's conclusion the sands are carefully gathered upon the buckskin or blanket that is used for this purpose. Sometimes the people present take a small amount in a little bundle to hang around their necks, but the Medicine Man gathers most of it. He walks first to the east, then south, then west, then north, and, finally, with a symbolic gesture, up to Father Sky and down to Mother Earth, he scatters the precious sands to the "six directions" from whence they came, or buries them, as the occasion demands, where no one will desecrate the altar, or the power of the visual prayer.

This is one of the most beautiful and sacred rituals of the Navajoo, for the Indian in his native state gives of himself with all his being. The love, affection, and reverence which he feels is made visual with a superb dignity, whether it be in song or dance, arts, crafts, or in silence. He considers it a privilege to gather together a harmonious expression of love, beauty, and devotion, consecrated and dedicated for the glory of honoring the Great Spirit.

A sandpainting could measure from three to fifteen feet, or more, and is usually done by one Medicine Man with two or three assistants. Sometimes visitors are permitted to join in the execution, but at other times the nature of the ceremony may be so very sacred that no one is permitted to see the sandpainting with the exception of those directly involved in the ritual of the ceremony. It is for this reason that an anthropologist may sometimes have difficulty in recording these unique works of art. Some scientists, however, have accomplished a marvelous feat of patient investigation, with considerable subsequent accuracy in reporting and recording.

A sandpainting, when done for ceremonial purposes, follows a completely different sequence than the same sandpainting when done for a public showing. The former is sacred and is executed with reverence. In the latter, occasionally done for exhibition purposes, color and direction both are reversed, and many variations brought into effect. In this way the sacred altar of the sandpainting is not desecrated, or the symbols violated, by a curious and non-understanding audience.

The presentation in this book, however, is based on the mystical, rather than the physical ritualistic aspects of sandpainting. It is an interpretation based upon my own observations, associations with the sandpainters, and heartfelt interest, built around but not taking the place of the rich gathering of previous factual information by those more learned. Advances in modern psychology are beginning to show more and more the value of this subjective and spiritual approach as a part of reality touched on by the subconscious mind, and of senses beyond the usual five. *

Of special significance to me are the symbols of the sandpaintings in their basic essence, which seem to weave a thread of continuity corresponding with the symbols of primitive people all over the world. An exciting similarity in meaning exists in other cultures in other lands, motivated it seems, by the very same reasons and purposes. ** Symbols bear mute testimony to man's attempt to explain the origin of the species, and the physical, moral, ethical and spiritual laws that man must use, know and understand if his journey through life is to equip him with the tools necessary for a higher and more evolved adventure. Through acknowledgment of the Great Spirit, the process is initiated by which he can discover his own soul, his own center. For therein lies the seed to the

*Parapsychology, by Rhine and Pratt. Psychology of the Unconscious, by C. J. Jung. **Religion in Primitive Society, by Norbeck.

understanding of the Great Mystery.

The sandpaintings photographed for this book were executed with a new permanent technique which I originated and evolved after many years of experimentation, and which is now becoming recognized through many branches of varied interpretative forms as a result of years of demonstrations and teaching in public. This new and permanent adaptation of the age old ephemeral art is achieved through the combining of a plastic adhesive with natural-color sands and minerals applied to a plyboard base.

My objective now is to return to the Indian, who is the source of these symbolic sandpaintings, this new medium of permanent sandpaintings for the preservation of some forms of his own native art. And it is my hope that all people everywhere may know more of the soul of our original American, through a better understanding of him from one of his oldest arts, sandpainting. In a forthcoming book, "How to do Indian Sandpainting", I will show how painting with sand can be reduced to a simplicity that even a grammar school child can appreciate after only one demonstration, as well as, in its more advanced forms, offering a technical challenge to the professional artist. Already, when introduced into school systems, sandpainting has served as a bridge for a deeper understanding between the red man and his white brother, teaching through symbolism the beautiful principles of the Indian, some of which nearly every youth group (Scouts, Woodcraft Rangers, YMCA Indian Guides, etc.) have adopted.

The Indian method of working loosely on the ground is an excellent medium for school pageantry, map making and such, in outdoor areas. Children are always fascinated with the gathering and preparation of the materials for these stimulating group projects.

Several Indian artists have indicated their desire to learn how to use this new medium for their own purposes while others have already adopted it. The acceptance of the individual Indians, and the recognition of the anthropologists has proven to me that this plan has real merit, and has given me the necessary confidence and encouragement to continue its promotion, so that both Indian and non-Indian youth groups can pass on what they have learned to their own people, thus bringing a greater unity and understanding to all.

The following explanations of sandpaintings of the Navajo, Apache and Southern California Indians give only the spiritual essence and are devoid of tribal ritual as much as possible. The latter is mentioned only where necessary, but generally the attempt is made to capture some of the intrinsic beauty and wisdom of a mystical people.

FATHER SKY AND MOTHER EARTH

(Surrounded by the Rainbow Guardian, see page 34)

 he first creation of the Great Spirit was Father Sky and Mother Earth, from whence all life sprang. The crossing of their hands and feet signifies the union of heaven and earth, bound eternally together by the Rainbow Guardian. Regardless of in which direction we may look, we find sky and earth fused as one on the horizon. The physical earth, and sky or mind (spiritual) must function together to produce new life. All things are conceived first in thought before they become physical expressions or manifestations. This is the meaning of the line running from the head of Father Sky to the head of Mother Earth. Therefore much physical pain, disease, or so-called evil, was first conceived in thought before it appeared in the body. To cure or treat the patient, a poor crop, or whatever the need, one must of necessity establish a harmonious rhythm with all unknown forces. "Let the wind carry my voice to the four corners (four dots in the painting), up to the sky, and down to the very center of Mother Earth."

The stars, the moon (sometimes the face of the sun appears also), and the constellations are shown on the body of Father Sky. The zigzags crossing his shoulders, arms and legs form the Milky Way... From the bosom of Mother Earth radiates the life-giving energy of the sun, bringing fertility to the womb of Mother Earth, from whence springs the seed of all living things.

Mineral, vegetable and animal, all things grow, mature, bear fruit (symbolically, in the mineral), and fall, returning back to the source from which they came (black oval at the base of Mother Earth and Father Sky). The mineral feeds the vegetable, the vegetable and the mineral feed the animal, but the mineral eventually reclaims the other two.

The four circles, in divisions of four, represent the four cardinal points of the compass, the four elements, the four seasons of the year, and the four ages of man: infancy, youth, maturity, and the transition age.

The bat, the sacred messenger of the spirit of the night, guards the sandpainting at the opening in its border.

Surrounding the sandpainting on three sides we find the Rainbow Guardian, with five projections at each extremity. Five are white and five are black, symbolizing night and day, darkness and light, evil and good, positive and negative, man and woman, birth and death, and so forth.

This represents the paradoxical world of this planet and all that is contained therein, which presents a constant challenge to man, as long as he is a part of this earth's vibrations.

The small figure on the left is an astral medicine pouch, deriving the power to heal from the constellations. Herein lies the saga of the Little White Beetle, a story that is told for the benefit of children.

The Indian parent never punished his children with physical force. To do so would prove that the child was already superior in reasoning power to the adult. When an Indian child misbehaved in the old days, the mother sent the child to the grandparents, or to an elder member of the tribe, for they, the old ones, regarded with love and reverence, had lived long enough to have acquired the wisdom to handle the problems of the small ones with dignity and love.

The child was first reminded that his erring ways were offensive to the Great-Father-Spirit and that the Father Spirit had a very special message for this occasion. Isolated by his playmates, who understood that the erring one must be left alone, the child would go into a retreat beyond the village where the Spirit would communicate His message in silence, for the voice of the Spirit is best heard in solitude. At the solitary spot of his own choosing, such as a high rock, under a tall tree, a mountain top (the place and the distance depending upon the age of the child), alone he must be silent and think, until such a time as the wise one came for him, or something of an unusual nature happened during his vigil. In any case, the child must observe nature in its fullest. Many messengers from the Great Spirit come via the little animals. Any of these creatures could be, and often were, Sacred Messengers. In this particular instance the little black beetle, commonly known as the little "stink bug", came and remained around the child for the entire length of his watching. Therefore, to the Wise Old One, the little black beetle had the proper voice. . and so we hear the story and "The Saga of the Little White Beetle."

"A long, long time ago when the Great Spirit first created the heavens and the earth, all creatures of nature were different than

they are now. The night sky was then a thing of far greater brilliance and illumination, with gleaming rows of well-arranged stars.
There were no constellations then as all the stars were so very well
placed that night was like day. The star light was brighter than the
full moon's, for the Great Sky Spirit had a very valuable helper who
took good care indeed of those wonderful glowing gems of the night-
time.

"This assistant, a very lovely and handsome beetle with a magnificent armor of pure shining white, was known throughout the
heavens and earth as 'White Beetle, Chief Star Keeper, Guardian
and Companion to the Morning and Evening Stars.' He began his
special job as soon as Father Sun retired to the home of the Turquoise Woman in the far west, and while twilight still lingered in
the evening sky. First he brought forth his great basket full of
stars, especially woven for this unique purpose. Then he would
proceed very carefully to place each star and planet in an exact location in the evening sky, beginning on the eastern horizon. By the
time he arrived at the house of the Setting Sun, the joyous radiance
of thousands of orderly stars illuminated the face of the night sky.
In this way never was there a moment of darkness or ignorance upon
the earth, for, without light, man is doomed to a limited experience.

"Those indeed were nights to remember; those were nights of joy
and ecstasy! Those were nights that thrilled the poet; those were
nights that wooed the lovers; those were nights of stardust and moon
song, of enchantment and delight!

"Before the breaking of dawn on the far eastern horizon, little
White Beetle would pick up his very special basket and, with the
methodical ease of a professional star gatherer, proceed to collect
his stars one by one, tenderly and efficiently cleaning and shining
each one before tucking them away. By the time Father Sun's shining face peeped over the eastern hills, little White Beetle would just
be finishing on the horizon of the far West. His timing was superb,
truly a professional job worthy of his long years of experience and
dedication to his task.

"But, as the years went by, with night continuing to be preceeded
by day, White Beetle attended to his precious stars with mounting
sureness that he was a wonderful fellow. 'Were it not for my hand-
iwork,' he would brag to all who would listen, 'the beauty of the
night sky would be lost to man, for is it truly not I who have created enchantment and the sparkling night sky which lovers adore?'

"One night, however, he was so greatly absorbed in expanding his own feeling of self-importance that he completely forgot the setting Sun, which had long since dipped beneath the western horizon. His audience, which had by now turned a deaf ear to his offensive boasting, had said nothing. With a start White Beetle looked up. Darkness was everywhere across the face of the land!

"Hurriedly he snatched up his basket of stars and scrambled in a mad rush to put them where they belonged. But it already was dark - oh so very dark - and White Beetle could not see where he was going. A few stars (which today we know as constellations) he managed to place properly. Then, oops! . . he tripped and fell headlong, spilling his basket of stars across the heavens. These form the arch of the night sky, which nowadays we refer to as the Milky Way! And, if you observe carefully, you may yet see some of the carelessly tossed stars which slipped from White Beetles' basket and form a trail of light across the darkened sky. But now no longer is the night sky like the light of day, even when the White Moon Princess gives out her full brilliance once in every twenty-eight days upon the earth.

"The Great Spirit had for long foreseen what was coming, but He leaves His children to work out their own problems, seldom interfering, unless called upon for assistance. Matters had now gone a bit too far, however, and White Beetle was called to counsel.

" 'My child, ' the erring one was reprimanded, 'you were indeed given a special job in My creation, a job well suited to your natural inclination for orderly and systematic arrangements. But each of My children have been given a special job to be fulfilled with joy. Each one of you have been created with special abilities which complement one another. I, the Great Mystery, have also hidden within the heart of each of you a challenge. There I have placed the seed which reflects Myself. Seek it, and you will discover yourself and see Me reflected in all created things. You will see me in the night time and the dawning, in the billowing summer clouds, in the rock, the tree, the fragrance of flowers, and the bird that soars in space.

" 'Each one of you also has been given the ability to reflect my qualities. From the Ant and the Bee People you may discover the talent of working. From the Flower and Butterfly People you learn of color, design and harmony, while the Spider People are master weavers. The rhythm of music can be learned through the voice of the wind and the songs of birds, in silver waters seeking a waterfall or in the murmuring of a sun-splashed forest. By helping one another and recognizing My spirit in each one of you, there is opened within you the secret door of your own natural heritage. He who serves his brother, also serves and honors Me.

" 'Can you not see, White Beetle, that your job was indeed important, for it brought inspiration, happiness and light to all living things, but it was not unique, for no one is more important than another in My creation. Only as you work together in joy and harmony without pride or envy can happiness dwell among you. By setting yourself apart you failed in your task, and, in so doing, you failed not only Me, but reflected this failure upon all of creation. Because of your conceit, the rhythm of the day and night has been disturbed. You have plunged the face of the sky into semi-darkness and made this a part of earth experience.

" 'Therefore, from this day forward your shining white armour shall be as dark as the night you made, and you shall bow your head in shame for the rest of your days. Go now, and tell your brothers for Me of the paradox force throughout My creation. Tell them that light and darkness are twins, like night and day, like man and woman. Inform them that the same fire which cooks your meals can burn down your dwelling, and the water that quenches your thirst is the same water that can drown you. The power which gives you life is the self-same power which will take it back. Your own thinking will guide your soul on the path away from Me, or towards your eternal reward at My side. Walk then the right path and be in perfect harmony with the whole spirit of creation, without pride and without foolish desire. There you will dwell where it is said: "In beauty it begins and in beauty it ends." The choice is yours.' "

*   *   *   *   *   *   *

Thus ends the story of the little Black Beetle, who once was so white, but is now commonly referred to as the "little black stink bug" (seen at the left of the sandpainting on page 33 in the rectangular figure representing the astral medicine pouch). It is not told perhaps in the poetic imagery of the Wise Old One counseling the erring young, but it is wise indeed to heed this counsel so that you may avoid the pitfall of the bragging "White Beetle," and never become known as a "little stinker."

THE WHIRLING LOGS OR SWASTIKA

(Night Chant Sandpainting, see page 35)

 ne of the most ancient of symbols, the Swastika, can be found throughout all the great cultures of the earth. To the American Indian it has special significance, and will always be found rotating clockwise, from east to west, in the natural orderly movement of the earth. It may be interesting to observe that in the late Nazi regime this powerful symbol was taken, tipped on its side, and spun counter-clockwise, thus creating a complete antithesis of all that is natural, and substituting order with chaos.

From the great center of life, four bars (elements) reach out to the four cardinal points of the compass, where we find Father Sky and Mother Earth sitting at the extreme horizon. Man and Woman (symbolically) have equal power of creation - the positive and negative polarity which, when brought together in balance, brings forth new life, light and evolution.

Mother Earth, in white and yellow, holds the keys that control the seeds of all plant as well as animal life; all things that grow, both upon the earth, and in the depths of the Wide Waters where new minerals usually come into being.

Father Sky, in white, blue and black, holds in his hands the keys that control the elements, the clouds, the rains, the thunder and lightning, as well as the secrets of the stars, the sun, the moon and the constellations.

The center of the swastika is the symbol of the Great Spirit, the Great Mystery, from which all things emanate. Here we see three white lines coming out of the center, equal at first but terminating in four different types of plant life. From east to west are seen corn, beans, squash or melon, and tobacco, the four basic and sacred plants of the southwest Indians.

The long white figure at the opening, represents the east or Sunrise people; the yellow-faced figure is that of the South People, the color of youth, spring; the red-faced figure belongs to the West People, those of the sunset; while the black-faced figure is that of the North People in whose control are the long nights of winter and the black thunder clouds that bring mighty storms.

THE TRUTH DIVIDED

 n the long ago time when the Great Father Spirit created the earth world, He fashioned it into divisions of four: the four elements, the four cardinal points, the four seasons of the year, the four ages, and, originating from the center, the four races of man. In like manner, the truth was bound by the four corners of the square. Each direction became the home of a family group, symbolically, not geographically, corresponding to the sequence of time: (East) sunrise, White-faced People; (South) noontime, Yellow-faced People; (West) sunset, Red-faced People); (North) night, Black-faced People. (Note: West People are turquoise-blue in some tribes.)

The necessity of each family tribe was the daily recognition and acknowledgment of the Great Mystery as they attended their daily tasks in harmony and peace. But, as the years went slowly by, with each season bringing forth different values in nature, as well as tribe (or race), a division in their feeling of importance began to develop. The rhythm in nature became disturbed, each season claiming to have the honor of holding the most truth, the secret of the seasons, the secret of life, and each tribe attempting a victory that would make the other tribes see the erring of their ways. Momentarily each tribe or season would appear to have control over all things on earth. But, just as the tribe of Melting Snow brought forth its quickening growth of the springtime, Bright Sun, of the summer tribe, would invade the land with blistering heat! Then Falling Leaf, of the autumn tribe, with great gusts of wind would blow the vegetation away, only to be followed by the Long Nights of the winter tribe who would overcome all with a mantle of ice and snow.

The rhythm of nature went from bad to worse. Strife, dissension, mistrust and seasonal wars were soon spreading over the four quarters of the earth (even worse than it is today). Each tribe was sure that their season was the "only way" . . . . . if only the Great Father would listen to their prayers. Tornados and torrential floods ravaged the land, angry lightning dissected the face of Father Sky, and earthquakes shook Mother Earth to her very foundations before the seasons were brought to humble submission and the arrogance of the tribes erased. Not until then did they remember that humility was the keynote, generosity and cooperation the melody, and sharing with each other the basic rhythm of beauty.

Only then came a Voice from out of the Great Silence:

"Listen my children: to stimulate your growth, quicken your inner awareness, through the observation of the changing seasons, and for the bringing forth of individualized and group expressions, you have been challenged. I divided the truth into four equal parts, and to each of you a portion of this Light was given. Like a seed of wisdom, it was carefully planted within the heart of each of you. Your first search is to discover this glimpse of the light within your own hearts, in your own minds, in your own family tribe, and in all things and in all peoples.

"Only when each of these four widely separated tribes bring their lights together in the center will each recognize itself reflected as but a part of the Great Whole. Then will the Greater Truth be known and with it the fact that in diversity lies strength when accompanied by that quickening force which recognizes in all things the same spirit flowing, harmonizing all the component parts into one master pattern. Then will you hold the greater discovery. With your hearts and minds impregnated with the light of the Truth of Oneness, you will truly emerge as the Elder Brothers, the Wise Ones, joined as one happy family, united and harmonious, with the Rainbow Guardian, symbol of abundance and everlasting happiness, surrounding all My family tribes throughout the four quarters of the earth with his blessed shroud of protection."

The Great Mystery seldom speaks to man directly, but usually assumes another form, often symbolized in Ceremonials as a masked deity (even here the true identity of the performer is concealed), for, in conjunction with the recognition and acknowledgment of the One Great Force, which flows through and is a living part of all created things, we must learn the lesson of detachment.

And we learn also that for each there is a season, both active and passive, in the rhythm of life. There is a time to speak, to work, to play, to receive, to share, and a time for silence and meditation.

BIG THUNDER

(Shooting Chant, see color plate on page 36)

ut of darkness came the voice of Father Sky and Big Thunder appeared. Lightning coursed the heavens in an arc of fire. Air swiftly rushed to the voice of Big Thunder and, blending with the rays of light, an archway of glorious colors accompanied the birth of the Rainbow Guardian (all the tri-color little sections occurring upon the bodies of Big and Little Thunders).

Twenty-four waterspouts were released from Big Thunder's wings; twelve spouts from each wing, symbolic of the four elements, the four seasons, and the four directions from which the "Little Thunders" (upon his body) can, and often do appear. These Little Thunders are the most able assistants that work intimately together, as is indicated by the interchanging of color on their wing tips, which guarantee a mutual cooperation between the directions of the four quarters of the earth and sky, as well as the four seasons of the year. Therefore thunder and lightning can appear in any direction, or at any time of the year.

The overpowering waterspouts on their wings are indicative of the tremendous quantities of torrential rains and floods which covered this globe in the beginning of time. Out of these waters, eventually the Earth emerged. Mother Earth was first created by the solidification of the minerals; secondly the vegetable kingdom emerged; and thirdly the first forms of animal life appeared. Big Fly was among them (the little figure to the left of the sandpainting). The Bat (at the right) who is a sacred messenger of the spirit of the night stands guard at the entrance, to the east. The zigzag arrows of thunder and lightning also guard this painting by forming a shroud of protection around Big Thunder.

The Navajo Medicine Man uses this chant, and this "visual prayer", to heal a patient who has been struck by lightning, or for someone who has been injured in some other way during a thunderstorm. The Medicine Man knows that there is a law of paradox that exists throughout creation -- the positive and negative forces. They are like the two wings of Big Thunder, mighty in their destructive power, but also containing much good medicine. Healing is possible when fasts and prayers are used, offering choice favors to the original

Thunder deities who did the damage, with the hope that these powers will reverse the procedure by bringing a counter-balance to re-establish the even-flowing rhythm of life in the patient's mind, as well as his body, paralleling the cooperative elements so strongly represented in this painting (psycho-somatic therapy).

Although it is not the purpose of this book to convince nor compare, but more to simply state and explain this phase of Indian symbology, you will note how "psychologically" and "scientifically" correct, and how reasonably and wisely used is the symbolism of the the Indian ceremonials.

The vegetable and animal kingdoms have a special language of their own, and respond readily to the influences of the elements as well as the power of man's thoughts. At certain times of the year when thunder and lightning ride the sky, supercharging the heavens with expectancy, it is considered a good omen for all of creation (as attested by science, which tells us that the ozone content of the air, so beneficial to health and agriculture, increases at this time).

Perhaps you have noticed how horses, cattle and other animals seem to be charged with extra vitality when an electrical storm is eminent and burst into jubilant capering and playful excitement. Their actions indicate to the trained observer that rain is in the air, even though the dark clouds may yet be too far distant to definitely identify a coming storm. Some animals head for shelter before a storm, while others wander far away from the water hole. Goats, in particular, remain close to water in dry weather, but disappear into the hills as much as a day ahead of time when rain is coming.

Almost overnight the mushrooms spring from the ground in the wake of an electrical storm. The Indian Medicine Man then goes forth into the fields to find useful herbs, mushrooms, roots, and barks. A tree section struck by lightning is of great importance, for it is charged with powers essential in ceremonials and rituals.

Even the ordinary house fly seems to behave differently under changing atmospheric conditions and particularly when rain is due and thunder and lightning fill the air. Big Fly is a legendary character of beauty ceremonials, and represents the spirit of all flies. In this sandpainting Big Fly is portrayed along with Big Thunder.

THE WHIRLING RAINBOWS

(See color plate on page 37)

he Rainbow represents the most powerful force of the creative spirit of evolution. It is the first visual manifestation of light and air, momentarily suspended in condensation of the water vapor in the atmosphere and resulting in a metamorphosis that brings forth the crystal liquid known as water, which is the very staff of life for all the creatures of the planet earth. The Rainbow is a major inspiration in most of the mythological and allegorical legends of the peoples of the North American continent, especially those of the desert areas, where it is always associated with water, the greatest problem of these arid regions of the west.

In this sandpainting the Rainbows are personified, with a clockwise movement that covers their appearing in the four quarters of the earth and the four cardinal points of the compass, where they may appear at any season of the year. The Rainbow Guardian's mission and his message are always the same: moisture in the air, abundance on the earth, new growth and new life forthcoming through the quickening process of the stimulating force of the rainbow colors that permeate the heart center of all seeds.

Therefore, the Indian peoples consider the Rainbow Guardian a good omen, and good medicine. Their headdresses and the painting of their faces for ceremonial purposes are often patterned after the rainbow colors. This direct and simple expression of childlike faith intimates the belief that if man patterns his life after the masterful manifestations of the Great Spirit, it is possible to fill his own existence with the same glory and the same purity; provided, of course, that he closely attunes himself with the clockwise rhythm of the earth, the sun and the stars. To do otherwise is to invite possible disaster.

When the Rainbow figures in some of the prophetic dreams of the Indians,[14] it is a good symbol, a reward that often comes to those who walk the Path of Beauty. It is the bridge between the earth and sky, and is both physical and spiritual. It is the ultimate unifying manifestation of the protective Spirit of Creation that surrounds all the worlds in all the planes of existance.

THE COMING OF AGE INITIATION

(Diegueño Indian Sandpainting, see picture on page 38)

 iegueño Indian Sandpaintings, made at Mesa Grande in San Diego County, California, although more specific in their visual content than those of their Luiseño neighbors to the north, have been discontinued for years.

This ground painting shows the sun, the new and full moon, and several constellations. The center white stripe represents the Milky Way. The large snakes are rattlers; the smaller ones are gopher and garter snakes. The spider that is shown taught the Indians how to weave. The mortar and pestle pictured contained a drink. The ritual that went with this sandpainting included the taking of a vision-producing weed in a drink called "tolache." This practice was sometimes fatal to the initiate and was, therefore, later abandoned entirely. The average size of this particular painting was approximately six by eight or ten feet.

At a certain time of the year, usually near the spring equinox, this sandpainting served as the focal point for the initiation of young boys into manhood status. The preparation for the young boys or girls was that of purity, chastity and wholesomeness. A prerequisite for marriage was also the virginal ceremony for both sexes. Even to this day, on some Indian reservations, these ceremonials are still effectively carried out.

Once a year those who had reached the age of adolescence were expected to prove their worthiness to the community. Typical of teenagers everywhere, they were eager to rush into adulthood. But it was necessary for them to show they were ready through acts of endurance, bravery, fortitude, resourcefulness and cunning. Outsmarting the animals in their own environment, capturing and outrunning them, hunting and providing food for the family, processing the pelts, and so forth, was each considered a noteworthy accomplishment. For the girls equally demanding tasks were expected. They were required to gather all the wild grass grains, acorns, edible roots or fruits, etc., and then prepare them for their daily use and for the ceremonials. It was also desirable to learn to weave mats, baskets, and all the other multifarious household duties that go into the making of a good wife and mother.

THE BEES AND THE FLOWERS

ndian legends, mythology and folklore, like our modern fairytales and stories of science fiction, although usually told as entertainment, often contain a kernel of factual prediction or meaning. But being out of time and place, like Jules Verne's stories, the Great Spirit uses the fertile mind of the story teller to project ideas, which otherwise might be rejected, except by the most receptive. Those of you who are already familiar with American Indian mythology and have read the many lovely stories written with sympathetic understanding and beauty, will remember many legends and myths that portray an enchanting philosophical and moral emphasis.

This same emphasis is present in the Indian dance portrayals of the creatures, such as in the snake dance, butterfly dance, deer dance and so on. Nearly all these ritualistic dances require the use of face masks, which tend to develop detachment from self as well as serving the function of psycho-drama by releasing pent-up energy and tensions. The painting of symbols and markings upon the dancer's face represents the most outstanding sense, acute quality, or power, of the creature portrayed. It is the essence, as well as the physical aspects, which is being honored with song, dance and gratitude to the Great Spirit for placing them here on earth to teach man. Aside from providing for man's needs, comforts and pleasures, they also share their innate secrets with those who are patient and wise enough to observe them. The Indian has great respect for the refined senses of his younger brothers, such as the sharp vision of the eagle that can see a rabbit hiding from a thousand feet in the air, the ears of the deer that can hear the lightest footfall, or the keen scent of the coyote hunting by night.

By acting like and mimicking these creatures in song and dance, the active participants as well as the observers, become more familiar with the mannerisms and habit patterns of each species. Thus a state of symbiosis, or subconscious partnership, unfolds and develops between man and nature. When the Indian is on the trail searching for game and food, it is therefore natural for him to become empathetic with the deer or rabbit, and enter into the spirit of even the herb or root, so feeling the movement or location of each.

The Indian permits all creatures to teach him on their own terms, in exchange for protective love, patient understanding and an equal respect for them. By so doing he helps establish harmony between the many species and members of the one earth family.

A fascinating investigation is now underway in many research laboratories in America, where more than 20,000 biologists are working with the science of Bionics, relating the knowledge of life processes to the solution of scientific problems. Here scientists may prove with facts that which the Indian has always known in the spirit regarding his little brothers of nature. There are many small secrets hidden in animals and plants, which, like the tiny seeds of the sequoia, hold a mighty potential. For example, the mosquito has a system of communication that defies even great storms. So far nothing man has developed is comparable. The bat's sonar system allows him to fly in total darkness even through a room crisscrossed with wires, and still not hit one of them. The sensing organ in the rattlesnake's head can detect temperature changes to one thousandth of a degree. Scientific studies have proven also that the rattlesnake has a supersensitivity that antedates the most advanced satellite infra-red sensing device so far developed by man. Many equally strange and yet untapped powers exist in nature.

It is little wonder that the Indian says: "Snake does not bite man, snake bites what man is thinking." When the mind registers fear, there is a definite temperature change, and by the same token there is also a temperature that is natural when there is love. The rattlesnake, as well as other animals, can and does detect human emotions. In the same way, the Indian is well-schooled in the art of empathy, and intuitively he contacts the feelings of all around him.

I once knew an Indian child who could hear the "silent" dog whistles and claimed he heard ants, lizards, beetles, bugs and all the so-called "dumb" creatures talk and answer one another, and he knew what they were saying. Like the Pied Piper or Saint Francis, wherever he went there would be a flock of wild and domestic creatures around him, all apparently enjoying a lively two-way conversation, often made merry with the trills of a child's laughter. His hearing range, of course, was rare, but not his relationship with his little brothers of the animal world. Among Indians it was not unusual to obtain a high degree of affinity and communication with animals, if they so desired.

When a colt or a filly is born, the Indian naturally has prepared a ceremonial ritual with the customary chant and blessing for the new family member. The offspring is ceremoniously given a name by the person who is going to ride it. The ritual is simple and direct, but the climax of the ceremonial is the breath-of-life given to the new born, wherein the name is whispered several times into the colt's ear. No one knows the name, except the owner, or the future rider. When this ritual is done properly it is stated the intervening period from the time of parting is not important, whether it be a day or a year. The horse will always respond if he is anywhere nearby. Although not necessarily in view, when his name is whispered into the wind, as in the same original ceremonial ritual that was first given to him, he will respond, and there is always much rejoicing when good friends come together. The warrior will ride and train his mount until they are blended into one being, like the centaurs of Greek mythology.

Jobe Charlie, a late Chief of the Yakima Indian Nation, told me the above story. Nipo Strongheart, also of the Yakima Tribe, had had such a relationship with his horse. When very young he was a bareback trick rider with Buffalo Bill's Wild West Show, and also served as an Indian Scout for the United States Army.

And what of the vegetable kingdom's super-sensitivity to temperature and light changes? Have you ever witnessed the flowering of an evening primrose? It begins with an almost imperceptible quiver which travels the length of the stem, pauses momentarily, then bursts into a little pouf of audible flower talk. In quick little rhythmic jerks the blossom unfolds to its lull-blown glory, as the protecting green calyx's sepals snap back against the stem. Watching this drama is like observing the thrill of a new creation or birth. The long period of gestation may have passed unnoticed, but not the dramatic flowering!

For several years I was with the Native Market, sponsored by private citizens and the State of New Mexico's Vocational Department. One of the Art and Craft projects was that of the native weavers who carded, washed, spun and dyed the raw wool before weaving it into rugs, blankets and textiles. This entailed many long hours in the field, collecting the flower petals of the chamiso plant to make yellow dye, walnut husks for brown, also leaves, barks and minerals. Each Indian weaver sometimes made his own vegetable and mineral dyes according to the materials which were conveniently available within his own neighborhood. The Chimayo weavers, therefore, might produce different dyes than the Navajos.

Mabel Burnside Myers of the Navajo Tribe is still one of the very active weavers and a master in the craft of spinning, dying and weaving the wool, using native vegetables and mineral colors. Several museums throughout the Southwest have beautiful dye card samples of over a hundred different colors which she has done. To name but a few:

Brown dye made from Rocky Mountain Juniper root, red rock and ashes; *Black* from sumac, ochre pitch and pinon pine; *Soft Light Green* from the sunflower; *Soft Pastel Red* from the red prickly pear cactus fruit; *Orange* from red rock extract; *Yellow-Orange* from Navajo Tea Flowers; *Yellow* from the bark of the holly grape root; *Blue* from the Indigo Bush; *Green* from the Indigo Bush and Sagebrush; and a beautiful assortment of others.

Although much of the knowledge of the older ones is unfortunately dying out, there are still a few who continue to follow the age-old Path of Beauty, giving to mankind a natural wisdom, which some of the branches of science are now at last attempting to revive.

*　*　*　*　*　*　*　*　*

The Indian parent ceremoniously teaches his child to observe all about him in reverent silence. The stern and balancing factors in nature are always present. The brightly-colored "lady bug," for example, will feed upon the eggs of lice and scale insects which are otherwise unfriendly to the good brothers and sisters, Corn Boy, Corn Girl, and those of the squash, melon and tobacco families. Or when rodents and other pests come to eat the crops, brothers "coyote, fox, falcon, owl and badger" are always near to protect and take care of them, each in his own turn and time fulfilling life's cycle.

The same principle of deduction was applied by the coastal Indians living along the rivers and seashores. They observed the spawning of fish and salmon, the behaviour of seals and whales, with a special awareness of bird life, such as gulls, pelicans, and cormorants. The Indians observed how these creatures trained their young to become expert hunters and fishermen through forced starvation. For the first three months the parent bird takes diligent care of the young, by which time the chicks are fat and sassy. Then the parent birds desert them forever, at which time they must literally sink or swim. The little birds have enough fat to last through a few days of forced fast, before they realize that they have to take a dive into the "sea of life" where, slowly but surely, they become expert air and water acrobats with their flying, diving, fishing and living.   Practically all wild creatures follow a similar pattern, with variations and exceptions of course.   Most primitive peoples through the world have been forced to adapt to the elemental environment by utilizing and superceding the mimetic technique.

In the primitive world it is imperative to know who's who, for survival depends upon one's knowledge of observation, identification and reverence for all life.   Everything that was ever created the Indian believes has a definite purpose and a message for man, whose duty it is to earnestly learn everything about his immediate neighbor and brother of the mineral, vegetable and animal kingdom. Whether it be friend or foe is strictly a matter of relativity, time and space, seasons of the year, or the ultimate motive or goal desired.

The ability to learn, to know, and to communicate with their wild neighbors on equal terms was noteworthy and to hear an animal call, answer in return, and have the game come curiously to see you, was a mark of achievement.   Many a good hunter has thrilled to this experience, but for the Indian the motive was one of deep reverence for his little brother who was readily answering his hungry need.   His purpose was not only for survival, but also for communion.   To honor him in song, dance and daily prayers, was to remind himself also that man must ultimately repay his debt to all creatures that sustained his physical body when he partook of their bodies for food.   Therefore, he also must be willing after death to leave his flesh and bones as food for the survival of the little ones of the other kingdoms.   This "law of diminishing returns" is still a recognized law of Indian life.

This is a law which, for everything you do (on all levels: physical, mental, spiritual), you must compensate, thereby maintaining a perpetual flow.   For whatever you take, you replace.   Whenever you receive, you give -- and visa versa -- for one who abuses this higher law, knowingly or unknowingly, pays compound interest.

*   *   *   *   *   *   *   *   *   *

Where better can a child learn about the reality of life and the origin of the species than by observing them during the reproductive cycle?   The Indian teaches a silent and reverent observation, so as not to disturb the animal's privacy.   It is an Indian law of learning never to interfere in the propagation of their kind.   Under no circumstances must a female be slain while nursing its young or when the cycle of motherhood is uncompleted in any way.   The Indian child observes the natural biological processes of all his little brothers of the animal kingdom, and accepts life and birth and death each in its time and place, as a part of the Great-Life-Giver's pattern.   In the ever unfolding pageant of the seasons, the spring-time brings about a resurrection of plant life to an awakening earth, and, in the animal kingdom, the miracles of birth.   He understands also, through the wisdom passed on to him by the Old Ones in cere-mony and story, that the act of creation is inherent in the seed, the cell, the egg, and belongs to the life cycle of all earth's children but that man is the only creation of the Great Spirit to be conscious-ly aware of his divine responsibility in transmuting this power and glory of life with a momentum of purity and love to the next gener-ation.   And the Indians have held this responsibility as a sacred law, from the most ancient of times.

The Indian feels deeply that blind passion and lust places man far lower on the evolutionary scale than the animal, for the latter follows the instinctive law of its being and is not endowed with a ra-tional soul. A personal sense of responsibility is inculcated in each Indian child from his earliest training, to be an exemplar, for it is expected that each generation should supercede in every achieve-ment the previous one. Should this fail to happen, then somewhere the elders have fallen short.

Absolute chastity before marriage was expected of both sexes. The body was considered the temple of the living spirit and should, therefore, be approached only with love and reverance.   Infinitely tender and understanding of the life within her, and which is born to her, is the mother who's mate surrounds her with the warmth of his love and protection.   Should either be missing, or the sanctity of the body be violated, then, the Indian believes, undesirable qual-ities may enter the embryo and perhaps seriously injure the new life, either physically, morally or spiritually.   Promiscuity was very rare in the Indian culture for this, he feels, is the mark of de-caying moral structure which directly fosters delinquency, disease, crime, and war.

For two individuals to come together at the altar of creation to bring forth new life was considered a sublime spiritual gift to be approached only with the noblest and purest of motives. This is a physical, mental, and spiritual prayer in action, and one of the highest forms of expression and communion which two souls may consciously experience together.   But it is a privilege which also carries with it a responsibility to the next generation, should new life be the result, and, therefore, through necessity, must be earned with chastity, and with purity of body, mind, and spirit.

Even with the changing times, circumstances, and the breaking down of the Indian culture with its principles, to which he so rigidly adhered, there are still four demoralizing habits (by-products of "civilization") which an Indian, who is yet on the Beauty Path of his own people, will not do:

1. *HE DOES NOT SMOKE:* This is part of the sacred religious ceremonials only, and not to be abused.

2. *HE DOES NOT USE DEGRADING LANGUAGE:* This coarsens the character and is unworthy of man's place in creation.

3. *HE DOES NOT DRINK "FIRE WATER" AT ANY TIME:*Alcohol eventually destroys the mind.

4. *HE IS NOT PROMISCUOUS:* As this dissipates the spiritual vitality and destroys the moral fiber.

Taking a moral census of the American Indian, using these four points, brings a realization that many have strayed from the purity of the Beauty Path and have become lost in the existing materialistic culture, as have indeed a good percentage of the general populace, regardless of ethnical background, who no longer recognize a "standard" by which to guide their lives. Thus we see about us a decay that could be fatal to our present civilization unless this process is reversed.

Prior to the advent of the Caucasian culture in America, the rigid moral standards of the many Indian tribes and the rigorous physical training and discipline of the red man resulted in a noble race, as physically perfected and as morally developed as any civilization which the earth has ever known. All peoples, regardless of background, need a spiritual regeneration that will restore this greatness of the soul once more, and bring it to ever finer heights!

The nobility of the race where "civilization" and contact with the adverse influences of the white man has not yet infiltrated, is still evident today in the integrity, honesty, sincerity, and both inward and outward strength and beauty of the Mayan Indians deep in the jungles of the Yucatan Peninsula of Central America.

CACTUS SANDPAINTING WITH BLOSSOMS

(See color plate on page 39)

e can classify this as a summer sandpainting, often made during the time when the cactus is in bloom, or in connection with the harvest of the pitahaya, or sahuaro cactus fruit. It is also made for the treatment of summer heat or sun stroke, or other mental fevers. Peyote, a cactus plant, may be part of the ceremony, given to induce dreams and visions, or to drive away bad dreams or nightmares. Although this sandpainting is made for the cure of certain types of summer ailments, the variety of interpretations for each symbol is left up to the discretion of the Medicine Man performing the ceremony.

The white cactus figure represents the east, the symbol of the returning sun and the birth of a new day; the yellow is south, or the perpetuation of life through the ever-returning season of the spring; blue is the west, the color of the Turqouise Woman's home; and black is for the north from whence come the long nights of winter.

The black border on the white figure, the white border on the black, the blue on the yellow, and the yellow on the blue, are symbolic of cooperation; the ability to help one another and to blend with the rhythms of the seasons.

The cactus blossoms indicate the power of the life-giving quality of the flower pollen, which is sprinkled on young maidens during puberty rites, or used at a child-bearing ceremony when the power and the wisdom of the unseen and eternal is invoked. The cactus figures are standing on sun dogs or spirit spots that control the growth of vegetable life.

Immediately below is the long black bar of mountain ranges where the Cactus People dwell. The small parallel bars of the various colors represent all the other vegetation of the mountain range.

This sandpainting is protected on three sides by the Rainbow Guardian who holds in his hands the keys to the elements.

The source and use of peyote and other trance-producing herbs, tranquilizers or antidotes, is often not revealed to anyone outside of the particular clan or secret society which administers it, and seldom to the white man who might subsequently pass a law banning its use.

THE SEED BLESSING WAY CHANT

(See color plate on page 40)

he personified rainbow, Natseelit, surrounds, protects and nourishes the seeds that give forth plant life, so essential for the the sustenance of all living things. Among the multifarious uses for this painting are a girl's puberty rites, house blessing, seed blessing, bringing rain and good crops, protecting livestock, easing childbirth, and the many other rites of family life.

The dot in the center represents the seed, the cell, and the egg. The four triangles immediately surrounding it (white, yellow, red, and traditional blue) represent the four elements. In close connection to these, the four semi-ovals in black represent the mystery of the night - the mysterious way in which the Great Spirit works the wonderful miracle of creating life. The beneficial powers of the rainbow encircling all, guarantees the successful growth of the seed, the egg and the cell. Each plant has three roots: one for each of the three kingdoms - mineral, vegetable and animal.

At the opening of the painting (east) and rotating clockwise, the plants seen are: Bean Girl and Bean Boy; Squash Boy; Tobacco Boy and Girls; and lastly, Corn Boy. All boys have round heads, and all girls are square-headed. As always in Indian symbology, there is reason for this distinction. The reproductive powers of the four elements are sealed within the feminine structure, although the opposite polarity is necessary to initiate growth.

The yellow bar extending from East to West and ending in white crosses, and the white bar going from South to North and ending in yellow crosses, are the four golden torches that emanate from the Great Central Spirit and reach out to the four corners of the Earth. From each cross is kindled three blazing rays, or the twelve sacred laws by which some Indian tribes guide their lives.

It is interesting that the Christ had twelve disciples, that the Sun has twelve signs of the Zodiac, that there were twelve tribes of Israel, twelve months of the Christian calendar year, and that the Baha'i Dispensation, as revealed by Baha'u'llah, has twelve great principles.

Big Fly and Mighty Eagle help guard the Sandpainting at its opening. The whole force of this sandpainting is directed toward bringing abundant food out of the earth.

THE CYCLE OF PLANTING

 ost Indian farmers abide by the cosmic rhythm of the moon, the sun, and the planets, and thereby plant and harvest accordingly. All grains and leafy vegetables, such as beans, corn, peas, melons, squash, and so forth, are planted in the full of the moon, while potatoes, carrots, beets, and the vegetables which grow beneath the surface of the ground are planted in the dark of the moon. Even though hundreds of miles from the sea, the planting and harvesting follows the pattern of the ebb and flow of the tides. It is interesting to note that many hospitals overstaff at the time of the full moon to accomodate the increase in births. Does it seem illogical that man, whose water content is even more at birth, and many plants which contain as much as 90% water, are affected by the gravity pull of the moon and the tides?

The Indian feels that the Great Maker, who purposely created all that is, impressed upon the plant kingdom a purpose far beyond its mere use as food. All things created have a language of their own, and the only way man can communicate with them is through reverence to the one central force embodying the wisdom to know, to do and to give forth life.

The Indian Pueblo dweller always had, and some of them still do have, extensive ceremonials of prayer and chanting before, during and after the planting of the seed. The seed is the beginning and the end (the alpha and the omega) of all life. The earth is blessed. Forgiveness is asked of Mother Earth for disturbing her rest, and all due care is observed to plant only holy corn, tobacco, squash, beans, watermelon and other seeds which have been prayed upon and blessed and are now brought before the altar of creation. Tenderly they are laid in the soil of Mother Earth. The blessing and cooperation is enlisted also of Father Sky, the Sun, the Moon, the constellations and the stars, as well as the little brothers of the underworld, to assist in the germination of this new sequence of life.

In the old days, before the advent of cars and pick-up trucks, the Hopi Pueblo Indians arose long before dawn and ran about ten miles to tend the Moencopi gardens and returned the same day, a round trip of twenty miles plus a day's work. They arrived just before

the first golden rays of the sun peeped over the hills of the eastern
horizon, and chanted the salutation to the dawn over the gardens, –
sacred children nurtured in the radiance of love, from the sky above,
from earth below, as well as man who is directly responsible for
keeping the balance in perfect rhythm.

Harvest time is a community feast, with prayers, thanksgiving,
and sharing with those less fortunate who are no longer able to do
their portion of physical work.

Many artifacts were made for the harvest ceremonials; specially
woven robes, blankets, baskets for winnowing and storing grain,
and special clay pots decorated with sacred symbols, each in accordance with tradition and ritual, for the Pueblo Indian feels the
harvest festival to be a special period of joyousness and the expression of gratitude to the Great Creator of life. The crafts are
the visual prayers of man, while agriculture is the combined ef-
fort of man, earth, water and air, precipitated through the grace
of the Most-Ancient-One.

The Indian tells a wonderful analogy of man to a basket. When man
walks the Path of Beauty with sincerity, honesty, courage, and truthfulness, he is like the upright basket which can hold the fruits of harvest and can receive and share the blessings abundantly. But when
he has strayed from the Beauty Path and is not trustworthy, honest
or reliable, he is like the basket turned over: he cannot contain, receive, or give of the many blessings of life. He is upside down,
empty, and useless.

The Indian basket holds a corresponding symbolic meaning to the
cornucopia, or "Horn of Plenty" of Caucasian culture.

Theirs is a different approach to a different culture, but the
basic moral, ethical and spritual values, common to most Indian
tribes, are still intact, as real as life itself, in such basic simplicity that most pseudo-intellectuals would miss them entirely!
Their culture is as old as the history of mankind, and the realities
of life will always exist to offer lessons as long as there are men,
elements, and kingdoms of being from which to learn.

"The Medicine Man"

"Father Sky and Mother Earth"

"The Whirling Logs" or Swastika

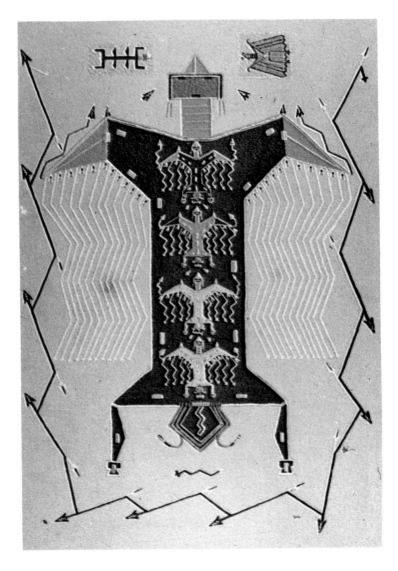

"Big Thunder"

"The Whirling Rainbows"

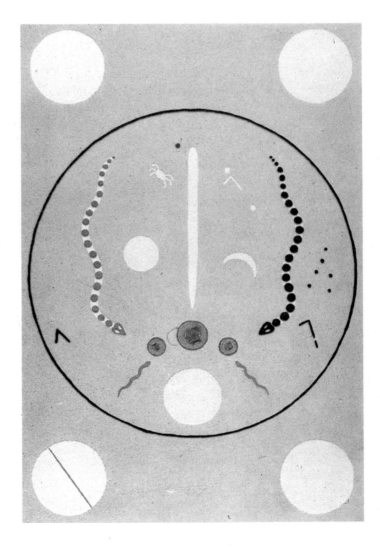

"The Coming of Age Initiation"

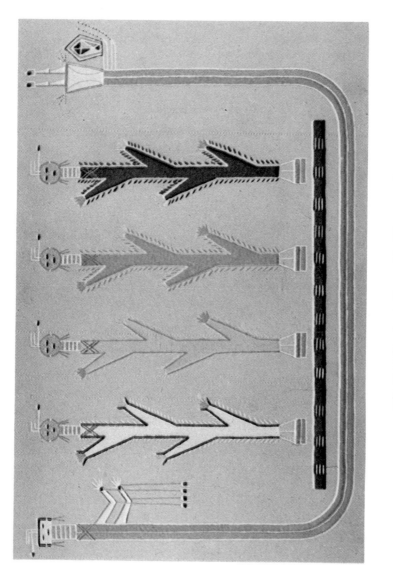

"Cactus Sandpainting with Blossoms"

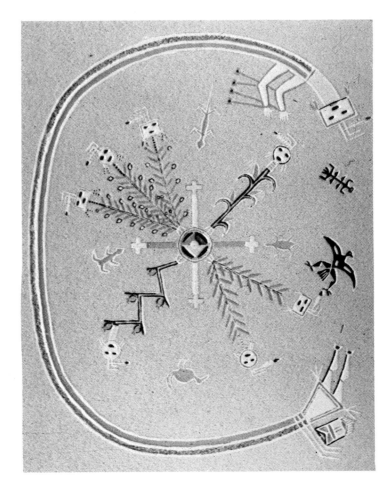

"The Seed Blessing Way Chant"

THE SMOKE PIPE CEREMONY

he seed, the cell, the egg, all need the warm heat of the sunlight and the quickening force of the four elements, to awaken the inner spirit that lies dormant within the structure of these basic units of life. When the sun shines upon the earth, the seed responds according to the memory it contains within the germ cell. The sunlight is transmuted into energy, and the seed begins to sprout; it grows, flowers, bears fruit, falls and returns back to the bosom of Mother Earth.

According to this then, when we look upon a tree, we should have the perception to see beyond the physical aspects and realize that the solid mass before us is in reality the spirit of the sunlight, stored and locked in the wood momentarily. But when needed, by the simple process of rubbing two sticks together, the friction will produce the needed fire for man's comfort and good pleasure. As the wood burns, the smoke slowly and gracefully ascends on wings of freedom, curling, spiraling and inscribing in space a ghostly prediction of our own soul's journey towards its ultimate destiny.

The pipe itself was a sacred ceremonial object to most Indian tribes of North America, handed down as a rule from father to son, and often buried with a brave and noble warrior.

The red stone bowl represents the minerals of the earth, while the tobacco is symbolic of the vegetable kingdom. Eagle feathers are often associated with it, representing all the winged creatures that take to the air, while the fire that burns within the bowl is the spirit of the Sun.

Tobacco is a sacred plant that belongs to the rituals of a spiritual ceremony, for, when an Indian smoked his pipe, the symbolic interpretation was that of the spirit of fire, light and truth. The smoke mingled with his words when he spoke, reflecting his inner spiritual illumination and understanding of this essence of the vegetable kingdom (tobacco), and was taken deep within his lungs, only to bear witness to his heart, his mind, his daily deeds, his actions and his thoughts before being released to the freedom of space. We can contaminate and pollute the air, the earth and the water, but fire is the great purifier; so, when an Indian smoked, it was only on those rare occasions when counsel was needed and his thoughts and deeds aspired to the purity of the fire.

The first puff of smoke was released down to Mother Earth, thanking her for the tobacco in his pipe, and for the many generous gifts of food and comfort.   Then he faced east and sent the second puff of smoke in the direction of the sunrise (home of the spring equinox); the third puff went to the south (home of the summer solstice); the fourth puff went west, to the house of the setting sun (fall equinox); the fifth to the north, home of the long nights of winter (winter solstice); and finally the sixth and last puff of smoke went directly to Father Sky, and the Infinite Mystery.

When the Indian Medicine Man goes through the sacred smoking rituals, the implications are many, but the symbology has deep spiritual meaning.   The ritual is performed with dignity, simplicity and deep reverence, signifying in effect: "I have spoken.   I have taken within me the spirit of the Earth Mother, the spirit of fire, and the light of the Sun Father, to testify that I speak the truth. May you also speak with the same spirit, and let the Great Mystery be witness to our council, that our peoples may be grateful to Him only . . . ."

The early explorers and pioneers, when first coming in contact with the aborigines of America, soon discovered that a prerequisite for communication, barter, or trading with the Indians was the ritual of the smoking ceremonial. With no understanding of the spiritual implications they went along with this "quaint custom" in order to gain the friendship and confidence of the natives.

A Spanish sailor, by the name of Rodrigo, who returned with tobacco from the "New World" on a voyage with Columbus, was accused of black magic because "he was blowing smoke through his ears, his nose, and his mouth."   The unfortunate Rodrigo was turned over to the Inquisition, the first victim of the abuse of tobacco!

THE FIRE CEREMONY

any tribes of North America have different fire ceremonies, the ritual and purpose of which varies with the tribe. One of the most remarkable of these is the one held to honor those who have passed the Age of Fire, nine times seven, or beyond. In this ceremony stones as big as grapefruit are placed in the middle of a roaring fire and kept there all day long. By late afternoon all that are left are live coals and rocks with the same cherry red intensity.

The old ones, men and women, enter chanting and shuffling their feet, proceeding clockwise around the fire circle a few times before seating themselves a few inches away, all the way around the fire pit, while maintaining the chanting tempo of the drum beat. Then the leader picks up a red hot stone in his bare hands and the others follow. They gaze at the hot stone as if in a trance before lifting it to the sky, then place it before their lips, pressing it to their tongues, to their eyes, to their ears, to their hearts, to their arms and bodies, as the rhythm of the chanting softly continues. The purpose of this ceremony is to prove one's mastery over self, following an exemplary life of worship, a life which recognizes with awe the divine in all creation. The old one says inwardly:

"I have lived a life of beauty, and as pure as the fire of life that has come from the sky above. My lips and my tongue have kept the silence of the spirit. My words have been kind and gentle and I have tried always to speak the truth. My eyes have tried only to see beauty above, below and all about me. My ears have heard the voice of the Spirit in the wind, in the song of the birds, and in His many signs. In my heart and thoughts I have held a silent prayer for my people, and with my hands I have created things of beauty. My body has been purified with bathing, fasting, singing and dancing, so that it may be worthy of becoming the Temple of the Spirit. Should there be anything in my body, my mind or my heart unworthy of this ceremony now is the time to purify it with the sacred element that cannot be contaminated. . !"

Strange to say, the old ones participating in the fire ceremony seldom ever were burned. It was a ceremony which those who had lived true to their innermost beliefs and close to the sacred traditions of their people accepted without question, for they had lived wholesomely and obediently over a long period of years. If there was any doubt of their truthful behavior, the result was painful burns. For those who felt that they were pure of heart, this was a time for proof, not with words, but with action.

When the ceremony was finished the stones were placed back into the fire pit, after which the chanting and dancing would be resumed. The crescendo of the drums and the singing would increase as they danced directly into the fire pit. Any spectators could later join in, going into the fire between the older people. The dance would continue until the live coals were stamped out with their bare feet, and only smoldering ashes remained.

There is a certain similarity in this to the fire walking ceremony of the South Sea Islands, which perhaps is held for much the same purpose.

The element of fire has a language of its own which the Indian appreciates and respects. That he excels in the fighting of forest fires the United States Forestry Department will readily confirm through the many stirring records in their files. To protect the forests and wild life and be always ready to fight fire, is an Indian law. This, in conjunction with their natural understanding of the harmony which should exist among all created things, enables them to be unusually effective in bringing the great element fire into proper balance.

An interesting story has been recorded of the first Arizona Indians flown in during the late 1940's to help stem a forest fire which was nearly out of control in Southern California. In the middle of the roaring holocaust the group of about 16 Indians stopped fighting. To the unbelieving ears of the forest ranger there soon came the sound of the rhythmic beat of the drum, and the eerie chanting and cadence of dancing above the crackling of the flames. "It's sheer madness," he thought, "for these crazy Indians to take time out for a waltz while the fire rages!"

As suddenly as it had begun, the Fire Dance stopped. With a few deft strokes the Indian leader marked a row of trees which were soon due to fall under the path of the flames. "Fire will not burn beyond these spirit marks," he said.

The red tongue of destruction swept to the crest. Then, under the bewildered gaze of the other fire fighters, the wind suddenly changed direction, leaving the marked trees only scorched as the flames retreated!

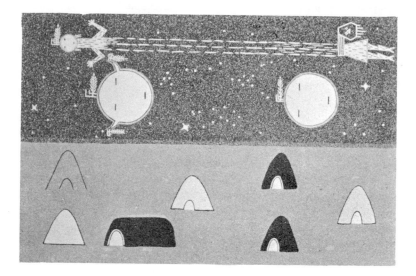

MOUNTAIN CHANT SANDPAINTING

uring the winter solstice, when the sun has reached the farthest point away from the Northern Hemisphere, the nights are long, cold and dark, and all of nature seems to be wrapped in a "blanket of deep long sleep." The ancients of many tribes had prescribed rituals to entice the sun back to the path of their homeland, these being as diversified as there are peoples. Of one thing, however, all were certain: sunshine and warm winds were needed once more. Among the Navajos this sandpainting is one of numerous visual prayers offered to the Infinite Maker of Creation to command the sun to return again with the Spirit of Life, bringing beauty and warmth to Dineh-the-people.

There are more mysteries in the night sky than there are blades of grass on the prairie in springtime. When Father Sky calls a nocturnal council meet, especially during the day (a sun eclipse), then the most able chiefs of the sky clan come to the great cosmic council to make powerful medicine. The elongated figure in this visual prayer is the Chief Spirit of the Night (the Milky Way).

Father Sun, with white buffalo horns, is the most powerful medicine chief of Father Sky's warriors, second only to the Great Grand Father Spirit. Mother Moon is the "White Princess" whose benevolent counsel has great wisdom. Her concern for her children is very obvious for she is present both day or night to attend to the well-being of her loving brood.

It is interesting to note that in some Indian tribes the men could not go to war until the women of the tribe held a council meeting where they would calmly decide if war was justifiable. Even to this day women have equal, if not more rights in the administrative order of the tribe, particularly where home and children are directly concerned. The Indian believes that the success of any culture can be determined by the position given to its women, and in the traditional Indian way of life her position was secure.

The stars and constellations are also in attendance in this nocturnal painting.

Below the horizon line Mother Earth has called together her peoples also to hold a sacred council with the seven sacred mountain homes, where the Spirit of the Earth People dwell. All of them gather together in the long house, or Medicine Lodge, where they can see and hear the mighty medicine from the big chiefs of the Father Sky Tribe.

In the blanket days of old in each Indian's work or artifact there was always one deliberate mistake, symbolizing the fact that we, as human beings, are yet striving while the Great Spirit alone is perfect. It is for this reason that one of the houses in this painting is incomplete, even as sometimes our dreams and visions are given to us only in part.

The original of this sandpainting was made on buckskin using sands, flower pollen, ground bark, corn meal and charcoal dust.

NAVAJO WIND WAY

(Wind and Snakes, see color plate on page 73)

 hen prayers for rain are essential, the snake is often portrayed. For, when the body of the snake wriggles, it is with the rhythm of the lightning, with the rhythm of the winds, with the rhythm of the elements, and with the rhythm of the rains and the rivers flowing out to the sea. The snake is, therefore, a very sacred little creature to the Indian, for, through its beautiful rhythm of life, it is the symbol of an intense reverence for the Master of All Life.

The snake represents the power to return to the center of Mother Earth from whence all living things spring. Here is the heaven of the Indian (below), for the rhythm of the earth we must know before returning back to the fuller freedom of the spirit in space. And it is the snake who is in closest contact with Mother Earth and can carry messages and prayers into the underworld.

The white figure represents the East, the home of the Morning Star where the sun is born anew each day; from the South, who is dressed in yellow, comes the summer and the power to grow; blue is the West, the turquoise palace of the setting sun at the end of its day's journey; and the black figure stands for the North wherein dwells the long nights of winter, and the Thunder beings who send us rain. The four figures represent also the four winds and the four seasons of the year, and in the hands of each are held the keys to the four elements.

The long black bar at the base symbolizes the Mountain ranges where the Snake People dwell. The small parallel bars on the long black one indicate the vegetation which grows on the mountain, and on either side is found the enveloping protection of the "Rainbow Guardian."

*　*　*　*　*　*　*　*　*　*　*　*

If prayers can produce rain, can they not also prevent damaging storms? How well I remember a personal experience a few years ago when Nee-Hah-Pouw ("Messenger of Light"), a Yakima Indian Medicine Man, was invited to give an Indian prayer and blessing at a Vedanta Temple located in the foothills of Los Angeles County, for which the date had been set weeks in advance. It had been cloudy and raining the two previous days preceding the final one, except in this particular section of the hills, on the Temple grounds, where the sandpainting was being made. Here, only a mist, like a heavy fog, surrounded us. The ceremony called for an outdoor setting, with a roaring fire to climax the benediction. The assistants were apprehensive about starting the sandpainting so early in the morning, as it would be fully ten hours before the completion of the ceremony would take place. The Medicine Man, however, reassured those present and recommended we proceed with the preparations, while silently pointing to a few birds, bugs and little flies around the immediate spot where we were working. "It won't rain in this spot until we have finished late in the evening, " he said, although a storm was obviously gathering. Flying insects, he knew, always retreat to a safety zone where maximum dryness will prevail, and quietly continue the search for food.

Reports were coming in all day regarding floods within two and three miles of us. Streets and roads were being "washed out" in many places nearby and we were apprehensive that no one would be able to get through to the Temple. We worked all day with the colored sands, finishing with cedar greens for trimming the borders of the ground painting.

Although the mist enveloped us all day long, there was no rain falling. The wood for a central fire was properly placed just as the guests began to arrive. Some told us of the difficulties they had encountered a couple of miles down the road where the water had tied up traffic, but, in spite of this, over two hundred people finally surrounded the ceremonial sandpainting. The fire was lit and roared skyward. The Medicine Man, with dignity and ceremonious calm, gave thanks to the six directions, with blessings to all, before unexpectedly saying, "It is now time to symbolically destroy our painting here in the outdoors and proceed immediately to the inside of the Temple where it will be safe to resume our story. The rain will begin in a few minutes. "

All hurried inside. Just as the last individual was barely through the door, a deluge descended, wiping out all traces of the fire and the ceremony. All were greatly impressed that the elements had so thoughtfully cooperated for this significant occasion in which one ancient culture was trying sincerely to understand another through the spiritual communion of the soul.

This is considered one of the highest goals in human relations, and is one of the reasons why the American Indian was always willing to listen to the early missionaries. When man needs to talk about his God it is a privilege to listen and is a high form of compliment to another culture. It is considered ill-bred, however, to attempt converting another to your way of thinking and worship, for each in his own way and manner must be left equally free. Thus many Indians have seemingly been receptive to the influence of the missionaries while yet continuing their own traditional patterns. The Indian nature is a deeply religious one, yet they may seldom attempt to communicate by word (apart from the language barrier) that which is the very soul of their life pattern, or even mention religion. In silence alone they communicate what words often fail to express. "What you do speaks so loudly I cannot hear a word you say!"

Many Indians are amused with the white man's Sunday worship, and sometimes wonder if his God is available only once a week. To the Indian every minute, every hour of every day is the sabbath, and all thoughts, words, tasks and actions are visual prayers manifesting the glory of the Great Spirit. It is interesting to note that even religious researchers have discovered that every day is the "sabbath" for someone throughout the world: Sunday: Christians; Monday, Greek Orthodox; Tuesday, Persian; Wednesday, Assyrian; Thursday, Egyptian; Friday, Turk; and Saturday, Hebrew, as well as for some of the Christian sects.

"Tapestries in Sand" is not presenting tribal religion, ritual or ceremonials, which are highly individualistic and vastly diversified. Regardless of the Indian tribe, or group, one finds that the American Indian always refers to the one obvious theme in their life: since there is only one FATHER SKY, and only one MOTHER EARTH all creation is related and are the members of one family. It is a theme not of separation but of integration, of the many individualized expressions of the ONE GREAT SPIRIT.

The reality is one, truth is one, and there is only one source of power that makes life possible on this earth. This is the purpose of "Tapestries in Sand"; an attempt to present the universality, the Beauty of the Indian Spirit; that which parallels the essence of all religions: the oneness of the family of man. All the Great Teachers and Prophets of God, from time immemorial have come to unify the peoples of the earth, and the recognition of this basic unity was an integral part of the Indian's awareness.

50

* SUN

ractically all the peoples of the world have at one time or another literally worshipped the sun. As a young boy I often saw Indians arise before dawn and patiently wait for the sunrise. All doors in the village faced east. Some Indians would stand silently by the doors until a golden sliver of the sun would begin to guild the horizon. A silent stir would run through the whole settlement, like a symphony orchestra responding to a signal from the concert master. Some would remain transfixed as if witnessing the miracle of a new birth. Others would raise their arms above shoulder height and chant softly a salutation to the dawn... A tingling sensation would finger my spine to the roots of my hair -- a peculiar, strange and expectant feeling that permeated my being -- like an inner music seeking expression.

Once I asked an old Medicine Man if he were a sun worshipper too. With his face serene, with the wisdom of his age, and undisturbed by my rudeness, he looked far beyond me, past the village and the white man's living quarters, and beyond the distant hills - his eyes and thoughts lost on the horizon of his dreams. We stood there for hours it seemed to me, for I realized then the confusion of my own thoughts. After a while he spoke - very gently, softly, almost like a whisper, as if talking to himself. In words to this effect he said:

"Does the white man worship the flag? I see him stand each morning and pay it tribute. Is it the flag he worships, or the symbol for which it stands? Man can live without a flag, but cannot exist without the sun, or without its light... We are grateful to the Great Mystery for sending us His worthy emissary to daily remind us that man is a child of light, and that we are nothing without Him. Therefore, we acknowledge His splendor by paying Him tribute at sunrise, at high noon, and at sunset."

SUN AND EAGLE

(Healing Chant, see page 74)

requently this sandpainting is made by the Navajo Medicine Man to invoke the lofty spirit of the Eagle in the healing of the body of a sick child. The child is represented in the figure of yellow - the color of spring - the beginning of life.

The blue background of the center circle is symbolic of the spirit of the sun, the spirit of the sky, and the spirit of the water: purity. For, in the blue we find harmony, constancy, and trust -- the poise and wisdom of the One invisible Spirit that surrounds and permeates all things. Protecting the edges of the sky-blue background and reaching out to the four corners of the world, are seen the sections of the Rainbow. This is the symbol of the combined powers of the sun, air and the water, which brings all things into perfect fruition. The crescent of the white and yellow, above and beneath the child, is the symbol of the union of the heavens and earth, "as above, so below."

There are twelve eagle feathers for each direction or forty-eight feathers in all. Each feather is for a song, and all the songs together form a chant. The Eagle is a lofty bird who dwells among the clouds and contacts the spirit of the heavens, for the Eagle alone can fly directly into the face of the sun, thus receiving the direct flow and inspiration from the life-giving power of the light.

As the Rainbow Guardian can appear in any of the four corners of the earth, we find it here in an enveloping shroud of protection; the threshold to the gateway of heaven and the everlasting happiness, abundance, and perfection of the Light.

* * * * * * * *

Found in some of the ancient and still well-preserved Pueblo buildings were small round strategically located openings. The principal "sun ray hole" was a small round aperture in the wall, placed in such a position that when the sun reached the zenith of the winter or summer solstice a sunbeam would pierce the opening. When this shaft of light, like a golden arrow, fell upon the sacred symbol, thus marking the sign of the changing time upon the land, it was then an occasion for thanksgiving, feasting and celebration.

In some tribes they used to weave rare harvest "sky baskets," with strategically placed openings forming part of the design. This ceremonial basket was used at night as part of the ritual in which the participant lay flat upon Mother Earth, with feet in the northerly direction, while bringing the basket to the face to view "the star that never moves" (the North Star), surrounded by its faithful warriors (the other stars of the Little Bear constellation). There were other harvest "sky baskets" also, used for observing other planets that had a special significance for the tribal ceremonials.

Most Indians were very familiar with the seven planets, that can be seen with the naked eye and have associated them with having influence upon the physical structure of man, animal and vegetable alike. The associated lore, knowledge, or superstition as the case may be, is little different than much which is found elsewhere in the world. It was obvious to them that the sun, the moon, the planets and stars had a definite influence upon the affairs of man on earth.

It is evident that without the sun, within a matter of days or hours most life as we know it would disappear. So powerful is the influence of the sun upon the fluctuation of the elements that even when building with steel and metals, engineers must allow for the expansion and contraction of the materials. That the Indian was aware of these magnetic powers there is no doubt, judging even from the ceremonials and rituals that are still in use today, incorporating the seasonal changes, even though intermingled with superstition. With all humility, and a definite conviction, he offers physical, mental and spiritual gifts to the Higher Forces that exist and surround him, believing that these respond as the rattlesnake does, to the negative-positive processes.

The Great Mystery has many ways to challenge man's thoughts, and offers many opportunities to learn cooperation, to develop and perfect his abilities, and to work harmoniously with these sky-rhythms (bio-cosmic) for a smoother, and better functioning physical world. Man's thinking process can help build a bridge of understanding between the physical and spiritual worlds if he balances his thought patterns between these two worlds in daily thinking.

This mysterious power is so delicately balanced that even a tiny feather dropped in moulting from a bird's right wing is balanced with one from the left. This manifests the great principal of applied aerodynamics, of balance and counter-balance, so that we see that the Great Mystery's glance does not miss "even the fall of the sparrow. ."

THE FOUR HOUSES OF THE SUN

(See color plate on page 75)

ach of the "sun shields" is stationed at the spring and fall equinoxes, and at the summer and winter solstices.   In many sandpaintings east is white, south is yellow, west is blue, and north is black.   In this sandpainting the colors are partly reversed.

Thus, at the opening of the border to the east, the sun shield represents the spring equinox, and has the blue buffalo horns of the west. The south sun shield, representing the summer solstice, has the black horns of the north, winter; while the west sun shield, representing the fall, has the white horns belonging to the east or spring; finally the north sun shield has the yellow horns belonging to the south.   Winter solstice thus wears summer solstice's horns and spring equinox sports fall equinox's horns and vice-versa.

There are many meanings for this interchanging of color in their horns, but, in this particular case, it represents the ability for cooperation between the seasons, the interlocking function smoothly flowing from day to day in a rhythm that makes barely noticeable the ending of one season and the beginning of another.   The tips of the horns touching one another symbolizes this even daily flow of life the year around.

The east shield has at the top and bottom a wide zig-zag stripe in black, white, blue and yellow.   This represents thunderstorms. The spiral on top of the head of the south sun shield represents sandstorms, whirlwinds and cyclones.

The west sun shield has on top of the head and at the bottom straight lines in black, white, blue and yellow representing the power of the frost winds, that make fall colors possible. The north sun shield has on the upper portion a yellow spiral representing whirlwinds of hurricane proportions, and blizzards. This shield has also four red feathers tipped in black, pointing to the four cardinal points of the compass.

All four sun shields have eagle feathers tied to the horn tips. This indicates that in spite of the potentially destructive powers of the cyclones, hurricanes, whirlwinds and blizzards, when men's thoughts are turned to the lofty heights, on the wings of prayer, thanking and blessing the infinite power that can display such tremendous energy, with true devotion and sincerity, this power can be re-directed into a positive and creative force. Does modern science and psychology seek for any different effect? The four rainbows or holy spots occurring in all the directions around the sun shields guarantee the beneficial end results; law and order have been re-established.

The outer circle of the pattern forms a mystic shroud of protection. There are four sets of feathers with five feathers in each group. This represents a different reaction affecting all plant life during the day and night, early morning (sunrise) and at sunset, as well as during the four different seasons of the year.

The opening of the east border is guarded by the bat, sacred messenger of the spirit of the night. He is in a field of yellow corn meal. To the left is the sacred medicine pouch containing all the medicinal herbs, roots and barks that the Medicine Man uses in his healing ceremony; all of which combined form a most powerful medicine.

CHIRICAHUA SUN SANDPAINTING

(Wind Way Chant; see page 76 for color plate)

he center shield, the symbol of the sun, represents defense and protection. The buffalo horns are the symbol of strength, while the eagle feathers at their tips stand for balance and justice. Be always ready to defend yourself, but if attack becomes imperative, may the thoughts of man rise as high as the eagles do, so that the motives may be pure and the actions shall be filled with justice and with honor.

All mankind receives the life-giving force of the sun (human figure in shield's center), without which all life on earth would perish. The birds and animals and all vegetation alike (straight green lines) are each individual expressions of the One Invisible Spirit which reaches to the four corners of the world, and each is bathed in the glow of the life and joy as represented by the individual "rainbows."

The sixteen feathers in groups of four, represent the four cardinal points of the compass; the four ages of man; the four winds; and the four elements; with each group pointing to a specific direction. The white is for the purity of dawn in the east; the yellow is south, from whence springs the resurrection of new life each year; the beauty and splendor of the setting sun at the end of a day's journey is represented by the red (west); and from the north (black) comes the long nights of winter and the Gods of Light and Thunder.

Among the Chiricahua Apaches, sandpaintings were usually done very simply with gray sand, ashes, coal dust and cornmeal, while the Navajos expressed their art through their additional many-colored sands.

The Navajos and Apaches speak similar Athabascan languages, and there is much similarity also in their cultures.

THE-SLAYER-OF-ALIEN-GODS

(Female Shooting Chant; see plate on page 77)

 hen a catastrophe occurs as when there are earthquakes, hurricanes, cyclones, wars, or anything that is not in the Path of Beauty and harmony, the Navajo Medicine Man invokes the Spirit of the Slayer-Of-Alien-Gods to come to the people's assistance and put an end to the calamities befalling man. SLAYER belongs to the beings of the Heavenly Concourse who are custodians of this earth planet.

The SLAYER-OF-ALIEN-GODS can produce all these things; thus he can stop them also. His body is covered with armour of flint, lightning and thunder, that he can control and often use with impunity. It is for this reason that we find him here in the harmonious turquoise circle of the sun. If he were on the warpath, he would be surrounded by red and black, but here the colors are under control, thus beneficial to man. Above his right hand is the symbol of the power to wield the mighty club to produce earthquakes; and in his left hand there are five lightning arrows to perplex the clever minds of men, especially those not having yet gained control of the five senses through prayer and meditation (indicated by five zigzag lines on his right cheek and on his forehead). The two feathers, one red with black tip, and one white, indicate the ability to use and direct the five senses with the sixth sense of intuition and wisdom, so that this God-like power is never abused, uncontrolled, nor deviated from the Path of Beauty.

SLAYER-OF-ALIEN-GODS is assisted by the lofty eagles standing on sections of the Rainbow Guardian. There is a shroud of bows, arrows and lightning guarding and guaranteeing the beneficial purpose of the symbology of these mystic and sacred symbols, that an alien power may not use them for black deeds. Man in his ignorance may produce earthquakes and calamities. A wise Medicine Man, therefore, never lets anyone desecrate these sacred symbols that have been handed down from the most ancient of times, for these symbols should be known only by those who have a song of reverence within.

SLAYER-OF-ALIEN-GODS is an ancient mystical symbol that also applies directly to the individual human life. For instance, as we come into this world, our five senses are the first big challenge which confronts us, and so it remains until the day we return to eternity. But, as long as we are children of the earth, it is our sacred duty to refine these five senses with an absolute determination to master them before we become victims of them. It is through prayer and meditation as practised in our daily lives that we can master and elevate these basic senses to a new place of thought and action where our god-like potentialities may be realized. Spiritually trained Indians and those who learn the secrets of self-mastery move on beyond the five senses into a daily recognition of the eternal and unseen as being as necessary to every human being as daily food. The ancient knowledge of what we term "extra-sensory-perception" was accepted by these mystical and self-disciplined people with the same natural reverence with which they accepted the ever-unfolding miracle of life about them. Prayer, to the Indian, is man's inevitable duty and must permeate every act of his existence from earliest training.

As the Indian "lifted his eyes unto the hills" and contemplated the majesty of nature about him, he saw reflected in every stone, leaf, and grain of sand, in every twig or blade of grass, bird or animal, a force embodied, and therefore an object of reverence. The elemental forces, such as water and fire, were regarded as spiritual powers. All things were personified, but secondary in nature to the one Great Primal Force which pervades all creation.

The power of thought is so great, the Indian believes, that there were no vulgar or contemptible words in his vocabulary, and undue anger was considered a sign of immaturity. There is an old Indian axiom which says: "Thoughts are like arrows. Once released they strike their mark. Guard them well or one day you may be your own victim." Even as individual thinking can effect the person, the family and tribe, collective thinking can influence humanity like a sickness (or blessing, if positive) and produce wars, pestilence, calamities and great destruction. For nature, the Indian believes, responds to man, and, like the boomerang, returns eventually to its original point of departure. When hate, anger or war is upon the land, the vegetable, like the animal kingdom, suffers, and even the crops sicken and will not grow.

Thus we are all potential Slayers-of-Alien-Gods, the peacemakers, arbitrators, preventors of calamity, the guardians of law and order and the spiritual values, against the evil powers of darkness.

RITUALS AND CONCENTRATION

bviously there is a tremendous advantage in self-discipline, especially when it comes to the ability to concentrate the mind's eye on a single subject. Even as the center of a revolving wheel seems to stand still with increased momentum, so are the seemingly monotonous Indian rituals, the chants, the dance, the single notes, half notes and quarter notes designed for the singular purpose of simplifying the discipline of concentration, the ability for which multiplies with repetition during conscious awakening: "Be still and know!"

These are training exercises for the awareness of the mind. The brain is the one organ that functions like a transmitter as well as a receiving set, and, like television equipment, it must be perfectly tuned in at all times. There should not be any separation, or wall, between the physical and spiritual worlds, the separation being one of vibration and frequency only.

The Medicine Man consciously knows and controls this delicate law of harmonics and dynamics with properly prescribed ceremonial rituals. Should the patient or individual participating in this ceremonial go into the state of ecstasy (which could happen with or without the use of trance-producing drugs, depending upon the individual receptivity) he would have established by now a conscious as well as unconscious protective pattern wherein the subconscious level could bring through, like a movie film reeling off impressions from outside of time and space, . . . a healing. . . a vision. . . an uplifting extra-sensory awareness, . . . or a transcendant experience. Yet, without the protection of prayer under the Medicine Man's knowing guidance, the scientific researcher experimenting with trance-producing drugs on his own without the knowledge, or pure motive perhaps, may produce extraordinary nightmares, kaleidoscopic visions and so forth but nothing really significant. In other words, the mind, wisely guided, may cross the shores of the unconscious to truth, where the unguided mind finds only confusion.

The danger of all such experiments is that the mind that is not built on a solid foundation of deeply felt ethical and spiritual values may become deeply shocked and disturbed by the turbulence and dark influences of uncontrolled forces that it finds in its own unconsious state. This may cause an unstable mind to collapse or at least find great difficulty in regaining equilibrium, unless knowingly guided.

A wise Medicine Man does not give trance-producing herbs or drugs indiscriminately. He must, and usually does, study the patient before prescribing the amount which can be safely tolerated, and then only after prayer and meditation have failed to inspire the desired receptivity, or the patient lacks the will power to develop concentration.

The will is one of the secret keys of the physical body, for once you lose the "will to do" you forfeit one of life's most precious gifts and automatically become a follower and a slave to your own passions. Our own society too often encourages over-indulgence of the senses by the constant din of advertising. Even such a mild trance-producing preparation as tobacco smoking becomes an increasingly deep habit due to the need to continually increase the dosage in order to maintain its effectiveness as a tranquilizer and deadener of the senses. Ultimately such a person may reach the point of choosing stronger habit-forming drugs in a further desperate attempt to escape reality, and thus another lost one joins the walking dead with the mind no longer captain of its soul. . . !

The ideal state for man is to live not by the use of tranquilizers or other types of self-delusion, but through the sheer ecstasy of spiritual inspiration. Man beholds the sublime through the unique and divine faculty of spiritual insight, a mystic meditation combined with a scientific concentration, through which a noble task, an absorbing hobby or even a daily job becomes so charged with all that is positive and vitally creative as to dynamically change the will to do into a sub-conscious and highly effective discipline. People with such a habit pattern may have dreams, visions and psychic experiences without the aid of any drugs, but rather as a culmination of the power of their love for the task to which they are dedicated. Their work is miraculously and yet automatically elevated to the rank of worship before the altar of creation.

Many scientists, painters, musicians and other creative personalities fall under this classification, but the Indian, before the too-sudden impact of a dis-united society suppressed him, often showed this creativeness and spiritualization throughout a whole tribe. Thus we are given the hope that this creative awareness, integrity and excellence may yet be rekindled and spread by a spiritual renewal to the bulk of humanity.

SILENCE

 ilence among Indians is that state reached when the mind of man is an absolute vacuum to the physical world, empty of physical "selfness." This silence is often referred to as the absolute self, or the divine individuality without a center, outer dimension or interruption. It is an ultimate in human achievement, since the disciplined mind must rest in perfect and absolute balance in the stillness that passes all understanding, before the right answer rushes in to fill the emptied mind with true knowing, or truth. It is an active detachment for the potential nature of self-awareness is still very close to the surface, super-sensitive to that which is near and minute, or to that which is as remote as the realm of the stars. It is indeed a paradoxical awareness gained only after long hours of rigid removal of the attention from the physical senses, until entering the silence becomes as natural as the act of breathing.

Silence is truly the language of the spirit among the Indians who feel that it is only white men who require the turning on of the "wind-mill machine", as I have heard them call the long-winded conversations of their pale-faced friends. Consider the awkwardness or even embarrassment which occurs in the non-Indian culture when two or more persons are gathered together and silence falls. Some type of verbal exchange is expected, even though it be completely without value. But the Indians of the old ways, who were in contact with the essentials of creation, could be perfectly at ease together in the silence, using only the waves of thought to contact each other.

Civilized man feels a loneliness and even an extreme melancholia in the jungle of the mind that may make stillness a terrifying experience, but he can pass through this barrier if he will learn to understand it. Then he would discover, as the Indian did long ago, that to stand in solitude on a mountain top at sunrise or sunset, or by a waterfall in some hidden canyon of ethereal beauty, and to absorb this majesty with utter peace and awe, in which the soul merges with creation, and self is forgotten, is to become one with a joy and happiness so tremendous that no mere earthly pleasure can compare.

Among Indians the fear of loneliness was dissipated by gradually training the young one to be more and more alone until at last the young initiate could be sent for days or even weeks alone into the desert, the forest or the mountains, and remain there without fear in silent and reverent contemplation of nature. This was a time for the individual to study deeply his own self, his strengths and his weaknesses, and so build the spiritual muscles to make his medicine (soul-power) too strong to be overcome by negative forces.

Almost from the beginning the Indian child learned a spartan discipline, but with loving warmth. A baby was prevented from crying by cutting off the air supply momentarily by gently clamping the nose (a matter of survival when hidden from the enemy). On the cradle board he was taught to remain quiet, and, when breast fed, his face was often covered with a cloth to prevent too much attachment to the mother alone, so that love and kindness could be associated with all creatures and men or women whose physical gestures and thoughts proved friendly. From the beginning the child was taught to observe in silence, learning that movement has a rhythm revealing the intent as well as the motive behind the mental thought pattern of any creature. Through his calmness he also inspired confidence in his little brothers, the animals.

While on the cradle board, with arms and feet contained, the baby learns to use eyes and ears to stimulate imagination. The singing, dancing and chanting of the parent both soothes and stimulates him, while the parent's pointing at or imitations of the sounds of animals and birds draws the little one's attention to them. Always he is taught to love and respect and understand his little brothers. Finally, as he grows older, he is taught that "man comes to fulfill the law of nature, not to break it, " and that he may now teach some other child the exciting game of observation, identification, communication and fulfillment with mother nature, who never betrays the trust of the loving heart, be that of man or beast.

After an early introduction to the many sounds and sights of nature, the instruction in smells and fragrances follows. Even on the darkest night one can hear and smell the "call of the wilderness." In silence can be heard and felt clear cut messages from both friend and potential foe. In silence is known their significance and reality.

The plant has a definite smell and taste, intensified when crushed between the fingers or touched to the tip of the tongue. The texture of the clay, the sandstone or granite are different than dirt or numerous other minerals or their mixtures. Some blind persons can readily identify even the color of a garment. Thus, through the steps of silent training and concentration, the Indian has fostered many of his seemingly uncanny perceptions, even in darkness.

During the initiation ceremonial the Indian father, or other older man, takes the teenager out on the trail in total darkness, and silently, the older one picks up objects and passes them to the younger. Both make a mental note of the sounds, the fragrance, the feel, and tastes of the vegetables, flowers, branches, roots, ground, and rocks on the silent trail. Upon returning to camp the young initiate recites what, where, when, and imitates what he has heard. Naturally his expert witness can verify his deductions. When all the initial training is completed, he is ready for the big survival test. His initiation rituals may be climaxed by spending up to three full moons (months) alone and away from his people. In some tribes the young adolescent would wear a loin cloth and a knife. At the end of this time his worthiness as a full-fledged hunter and warrior could be judged by the materials, in the way of garments, pelts, bows and arrows, and so forth, that he brought back with him.

His honor was much greater if all he accomplished was done without contact with any human soul, friend or foe. The more remote his austerity the greater his potential as a true leader, for the original Indian training spelled awareness that leadership is of necessity a lonely life, one of decisions and responsibilities. The earlier this spartan training began, the better the opportunity to discover the true self of the individual. The personality, like a flower, must burst into the fullness of its springtime potential and be exposed to the high noon sun of tests and difficulties. Silence and solitude endured under the handicap of suffering and forced limitation, makes the initiate find and rely upon his own moral strength. Only through fortitude, perseverance, endurance, keen observation, resourcefulness, ingenuity, swiftness, and, above all, friendly and generous understanding with all beings, can he emerge from such an ordeal. The best Indian scouts came out of this masterful type of training with the marked ability to readily read the book of life before them, and, in turn, leave some imprints of their own upon the trails of time. They were indeed the masters of what we moderns term: visual education!

One of the most vital items an Indian brought back from this experience was his Medicine, often a small bag or bundle filled with

things he felt were important reminders of the trip, or which entered
into his dreams. Such things might include a buckskin bag of soil,
an eagle feather, a bit of mountain mahogany bush bark or a sumach
leaf. These, in his later years, he would often lift to his nose to
smell, and the rich aroma, filled with deep memories of his first
true awakening to the meaning of life, would give him renewed
strength and moral courage to meet and understand his difficulties.

Whenever one or more Indians departed on a long and perilous
journey, there was always one or more elders who volunteered to
remain in the Medicine Lodge and keep the vigil of the mystic silence, when the "twin self" (soul) went on a "spiritual journey" (as-
tral-projection). These people of vision chant and pray constantly
for the success of the initiate, or the expedition. Between, there
are long periods of absolute trance-like silence, when their eyes
dreamily close with a steady focus upon the slowly burning fire in
the center of the lodge. The physical bodies are present, but their
minds and thoughts are far away with the wandering kinsmen, ready
to protect them with a loving and prayerful spirit.

Without a word, those left behind in camp or in the village, could
also know what was going on far away, for they could see the white
smoke coming up from the Medicine Lodge, and, as long as it was
white, the omen was good. But, if it should become black or fail to
rise altogether, then there would be another sad story to tell. Other parents, from many places, whose beloved sons have been far
away in a war, have kept similar vigils of prayer and they too may
have sometimes sensed what has happened to their loved ones.

At sunset or at sunrise, sometimes there would be a "bulletin"
forthcoming from the medicine lodge in the form of a chant. If one
would listen carefully, or pay very close attention to the smoke sig-
nals, the silent puffs eloquently conveyed the messages to everyone.
These venerable ones, sitting serenely in trance, would take turns
chanting the story of the absent clansmen while ceremoniously drop-
ping bits of fragrant green incense herbs into the fire which would
turn into voluminous white smoke, controlled by a small ceremonial blanket woven especially for the occasion.

These descriptive visions, with their many witnesses, were ver-
ified later on when the absent members returned to camp. These
so-called para-normal or extrasensory perceptive experiences of
the American Indians are readily acceptable as the normal experience of all those dedicated souls who walk the Beauty Path.

When the Twin Self (soul) goes on a   Spirit Journey, it enters into what has been called the fourth-dimensional plane, an awareness where one can feel, see and know or have rapport (spiritual connection) with plants, animals and people at once . . . !   Your soul is of that single element in unity with the spirit (reality) of all things. (Science has proven the interchangeability of all the atoms in all the kingdoms.) The spirit can be everywhere at any given time   at once, and the mind open to that mirroring reality, can go away through rocks and mountains or into the roots, branches and flowers of the plant. What or who one "sees" in this spirit vision may as well be encased in pure crystal, for there is nothing hidden in body, mind or thought.   There is oneness everywhere, no separation or division by time or space. This is what some American Indians call "Orrenda" - affinity, universal rapport, oneness, all words being limited in comparison to the comprehensive interpretation of their meanings.   These spiritual qualities of the silence, developed through the harmonious kinship with all life, augmented by prayer, meditation and fasting, are truly a part of the silent "Path Of Beauty. "

*   *   *   *   *   *   *   *   *   *

Our 115 year old friend, Tatzumbie du Pea, from the Paiute Indian Tribe, has told us many wonderful stories of her life. One, among many, concerns her great grandchildren. Whenever these children misbehaved she would give them fair warning that she would "go away" if they persisted. If they did not obey her promptly, she would completely ignore them, not speaking, nor even moving, but remaining in the trance-like state of a "wooden Indian. " The children would soon come to the realization that Gramma had "gone away. "

"Gramma is not here, " they would say sadly to each other. "We should have obeyed. Now she is gone, and Gramma can tell the funniest stories!"

Very apologetically then they would come to her. "We are very sorry, Gramma, and hope you will come back soon. "

Following this apology, Gramma might wait for a time before returning from her absent-silent-state, to find the repentant children moving about as quiet as little mice.

Many Indians are capable of this type of passive withdrawal when approached condescendingly by someone. Indians are taught to be polite, but, if pressed by circumstances, they will withdraw, and, even though they may be able to speak English, an interpreter must be found for communication. I have known of anthropologists doing research, who treated these people like backward children. Consequently the Indian did nothing to change this opinion, with the subsequent published manuscripts perpetuating a misunderstanding.

The ability to "turn themselves off" is so remarkable among some Indians that the lie-detector apparatus registers on them almost at a standstill, and many have had operations and teeth drilled without anesthesia, relying on their ability to withdraw completely. A few years ago a psychiatrist ran into a dozen or so Indians from a reservation who were brought to a California hospital. Not understanding the Indian and his trained ability to retreat into the silence, he diagnosed them as "having catatonic schizophrenia! " *

* * * * * * * * *

The Indian feels that when an orator delivers a truly inspired discourse, nodded heads during the speech show he is deeply touching his audience, but the greatest tribute that can be paid him is an absolute aftermath of silence, as, in their hearts, the listeners continue to follow him devotedly on the pathway he has led them. The rude crash of applause is a shattering force, breaking the timeless spell.

A wonderful experience and a rare privilege to witness among some American Indians, is when a member of the immediate family, a beloved friend, or two young lovers return home after a long separation, and finally coming before each other, are transfixed in a sweet silence, savoring the ecstasy of unquenchable delight. . . ! They let their spirits dance to the rhythm of their thoughts for a long while before the silence is broken. . .

* * * * * * * * *

A personal experience with One—Who—Knew—The—Silence.

As a young artist, many years ago, I edged my way through the milling throng at a Los Angeles County Fair in Pomona, with an unexplainable feeling of mounting anticipation. I was drawn as by a magnetic force to one spot on the grounds. Here would be a Navajo Medicine Man making one of the very rare ceremonial Sandpaintings ever done before the public.

*This incident was reported in a lecture given on Febuary 17, 1959 at Boston University on "Navajo Indian Paintings: Symbolism, Artistry, and Psychology, " by Leland C. Wyman, Ph. D.

As I hurried along, my memory slipped back to embrace those years I had lived among the Indian peoples. It was then that I had first watched the Navajos make their sacred Sandpaintings. Touched by the depths and magnitude of the philosphy embodied in this transitory art, the flame of inspiration had been kindled in me to someday make this beauty permanent. But long years of experimentation followed before this ideal became visible.

I gripped more tightly the flat brown parcel beneath my arm, for it held silent testimony to the realization of this dream within me. With a plyboard base and plastic adhesive, those ephemeral sands of natural color at last had formed a bond of permanence. It was a good feeling to know that, through recognition of this new medium and technique, my first one-man show was then scheduled for exhibition in New York's American Museum of Natural History. But most important of all to my young heart was that this new art form, the inspiration for which I had received from the Indian, be approved and used by the Indian himself. . . In only a few more yards I would meet a Medicine Man straight from the heart of the Navajo country!

For a moment I paused in the doorway. On every side of this large well-lit room were Indians of the Southwest, brought direct from the reservation under the sponsorship of the Fair Association to display and demonstrate their native arts and crafts. These silent and colorfully costumed people were busily at work at the loom, basket-making, silver working, fashioning leather objects and painting. In the very center of the room was a fenced off area about twelve feet square surrounded by a horde of onlookers. There sat a venerable Navajo Medicine Man "painting" loosely upon the silken sands the age-old traditional symbols of the Living Spirit. The looks of wonderment on every hand, however, revealed plainly that there were few who realized that sandpainting is a very old Indian art, or that it has a special and sacred significance.

For many hours the old Navajo sat silently upon the sand in Buddha fashion, evolving a design of unbelievable precision and beauty. All day long I kept hoping for the opportunity to speak with him. But the Indian knows that the language of the spirit is silence. In silence he always makes the Sandpainting, for the Sandpainting itself is a visual prayer, and one should not interrupt a prayer with words.

At last, after six and a half hours, there came the long-awaited moment. Slowly he rose and left the arena for his one "break" of

the day. Momentarily the crowd which had surrounded him dissipated as if by command. Returning, he paused for an instant at the
fence. In a flash I was behind him. Briefly I spoke of the beauty
of the Sandpainting and what it had meant to me, and asked him to
view my own permanent sample. Regal as a flute, the old Medicine Man stood listening. Without a flicker of change in expression, he nodded only in assent. And still without turning he took
the painting into his hands and looked at it long, in silence.

For me, what followed was a moment of magic. The encroach-
ing crowd seemed to recede into nothingness, and there hovered a
sense of expectation that was transcendental. For a brief moment
the serene features of that bronzed old Indian were an embodiment
of a whole proud people, a magnificent race, who had understood
the silence, and had been rewarded by its priceless secrets.

A slender dark sensitive finger began to move. With delibera-
tion it touched a tiny raised dot upon the surface. The other fingers joined in, and, held just a fraction above the painting itself,
they patterned a circle all the way around - - clockwise, slowly,
silently, back to the very beginning.

Only then did the old man turn to me. The radiance of the sun
bursting from behind a cloud was in that smile, and, in the calm
dark eyes shone knowingness and wisdom . . . My heart sang with
joy, for, through this moment in which I had been accepted fully
and completely, I had felt the pulse beat of the infinite. Through
the old Medicine Man, who had consciously attuned himself to the
language of the spirit in silence, there had been given back from
out of the silence a speech more eloquent than could ever be spoken!

As all of us impregnate that which we do with that which is our-
selves, the Medicine Man was, in reality, picking up the vibrations
from the painting and registering them in his own keenly attuned
awareness. Through his sensitive fingertips he had contacted my
spirit and knew my innermost feelings, integrity, and the motive
which lay behind.

Even as radio, which is a man-made instrument, can pick up
the fine vibrations from out of the ether and translate them into
meaning, why should not we, who are much finer instruments,
fashioned by the Maker-of-All, clear our channels like this old Indian, and register the greater and more subtle vibrations ?

*   *   *   *   *   *   *   *   *   *

There are those who do not recognize the paranormal qualities of extra-sensory perception, and yet they are common between many husbands and wives, brothers and sisters, and those who are very close to each other. How very great is the seed of potential within each of us, were it but recognized, disciplined, developed, and attuned!

Does it seem surprising that on meeting an Indian by chance in the desert he might tell you that your visit had been expected for some time, state briefly long forgotten incidents from your past, and conclude with a prediction for the future? Following several such experiences on the Navajo Reservation, I had the eerie feeling that nothing one ever does is hidden from some people, and my admiration and respect for these rare ones has increased with the years.

My earliest childhood recollection of psychic phenomena was at the age of about four and a half. It was early morning and my mother and I were alone in the house. Standing near to her, my mouth was expectantly watering with hunger as she stood by the kitchen stove frying an egg for breakfast. As she lifted the pan and turned to place the egg on my plate, she suddenly dropped the utensil with eggs and all, and ran towards the outside door, crying, "Mi hijo, mi hijo" ("my son, my son")! I ran after her screaming without knowing why.

Outdoors I could see nothing, nor could she. After an hour or more, my twelve year old brother was brought in with a bullet through his head, killed in a hunting accident a few miles from home at the moment my mother had dropped the egg, and cried out "Mi hijo!" From out of the silence he had come to mother to say farewell . . .

Disturbed by my family's mourning, and desperate to get away, I ventured outdoors for the first time that day, into the early evening twilight. In my deep childish grief I wanted to be alone. Boldly I walked an enormous distance into the unknown, in my own backyard, sat on top of a pile of broken adobe, and sobbed. I soon became aware that I was not alone. There was someone, or something, keeping a sympathetic rhythm to my laments. Flattered that someone cared this much, I eagerly began to search around me for the source. Filled with disappointment, I looked above, and, with unbelieving eyes, beheld a single, lonely twinkling star that seemed to rhythmically harmonize to the deep hurting inside of me. With my childish sympathy I felt sorry for the poor thing up there in the big empty twilight sky. The song of the star was suddenly voiced in the chirp of the cricket at my side, bridging earth and sky into one and enfolding me in the warm feeling that my brother was not lost.

HYPNOTHERAPY AND HEALING

mong the American Indians, the truly successful Medicine Man uses a seemingly hypnotic stimulus consciously directed at the seven major physical glands (or psychic centers) by exciting the activity of the five senses. By carefully controlling the balance of the body and mind, with the judicial use of the four primary elements and the three kingdoms (see page 26), and the application of a stimulating environment of sound, sight, smell, taste and feeling, he guides all the materials, elements and forces of the body, mind and soul of the patient toward healing. It goes without saying that the older the Medicine Man the greater should be his esteem and prestige, if he has been proven successful in his past performances. The wisdom of the ages is at his disposal in both the physical as well as the spiritual worlds, for he has already arrived at his own psychic centers, and understands the infinite inter-play of cosmic forces in body and mind.

The picturesque sandpainting first enchants the *sense of sight,* with the mineral, vegetable and animal kingdoms represented in the painting. This symbolism, as well as the sequence that follows, is often adhered to even among the non-sandpainting tribes. Therefore, the ritual of the prayerful "sing" or "chant" in all tribes has an affinity to the rhythm of a primitive lullaby, awakening an ancient reverie of the long ago through the *sense of hearing.*

The patient helps to paint with sand, if he is able, but finally sits in the center of the sandpainting, or equivalent symbolism. In some tribes the chosen spot is a ceremonial blanket, or holy ground. Feathers, usually eagle, are most effectively and dramatically used by the Medicine Man, who, from time to time, gently touches the patient for the physiological as well as psychological impact, taking him by surprise with this soft eerie contact to arouse the *sense of touch.*

Sweet smelling herbs are ceremoniously placed in the sacred fire, where the smoking incense intensifies the awareness of the *sense of smell,* and deep within the lungs the air carries the fragrant message to every living cell.

Carefully prepared teas made from spring water, or melting snows are given, or herbs, jimson weed, peyote, mushrooms or whatever the Medicine Man deems necessary to activate the *sense of taste*. All is done in accordance with tradition, location and time of year, depending on the particular tribal custom. The ultimate purpose is that not a single creation of the Great Spirit is left without being duly recorded and acknowledged with utmost reverence and devotion. The full power of the mystical rhythm of such a ceremony is felt by all sincere initiates, who entertain no doubt as to the final esoteric impact.

This type of ancient hypnotherapy has yet to produce a negative side effect, for its cadences are based on the attributes of the positive-negative equanimity or balance of the mystagogue conducting the sacred ceremony.

During the ceremony the patient becomes the apex of the whole cosmos, and, amidst the outpouring of loving attention, he becomes the center of the circle of prayer, the object of adoration at the sacred altar of creation. He is, thereby, made whole again, for it is done unto him as he believes. -- If his faith is that of the mustard seed, the end result may be miracle-therapy. . !

This is briefly, in essence, but a small indication of the intricate ancient tribal rituals that have been part of this continent for centuries, and where, in spite of all our technical advances, there have been only a handful of people attuned to investigate these potentials for the benefit of mankind. It is only of late that scientists, and a few advanced ones in the healing arts, are finally discovering another key from the Indian Medicine Man's "magic cures."

Hypnosis often produces a cure because the strong will of the operator commands, controls, and directs the mind into a specific channel of behavior. However, patients have been known to develop even more serious conditions as an aftermath than the original affliction, for the old subconscious escape-valve was permanently blocked before finding a satisfactory substitute for the attention-focusing-factors behind the original malady. *

Often a patient, like a small child, and usually in his subconscious mind, does not want to be weaned from a psychic illness because he is still attached to his mother through the psychic chord in a symbolic manner. Hypnotism may effect a temporary cure only to see the patient relapse into a different sort of disease in his

*Hypnosis in Modern Medicine, 3rd Edition, by Jerome M. Schneck. 1963, C. C. Thomas.

desperate search for the illusion of security in self-gratification.

If you are familiar with the hypnosis technique you will be immediately aware that the Indian Medicine Man does not use the suggestive approach for producing a trance. He uses no direct or even indirect words, instructions or suggestions at any time. Prayer, chanting and the prescribed rituals are his technique. This is something entirely different from hypnosis, inasmuch as the patient responds to an inner stimulus activated by the vibratory chanting and prayer patterns through the Medicine Man, whereby the state of consciousness is raised to higher planes.

Since the healing of the patient is an act of faith, we may profitably compare the patient to the average musician who suddenly comes under the expert direction of a good conductor's baton. Because of his previous disciplinary training, combined with obedience to the inspired master, plus his own faith and knowledge of the musical rhythm, the musician is able to faithfully follow the slightest swing and sway of the baton, with his own inner rhythm synchronized in perfect accord to the symphony. From this he gains a feeling of inner tranquillity and vibrant growth which combined produces an extraordinary joy.

This type of conditioned receptivity could, at times, be influenced by the slightest therapy, whether it be hypnosis or a form thereof, a metaphysical treatment, or just a parasympathetic encouragement. All would have a positive effect in healing the patient.

Each Medicine Man is an individual and his particular background, including the rituals peculiar to his tribe, his own special training, and, above all, his reputation as a successful healer, are necessary to know before the true picture comes into focus. Very often these people have a specialty and everyone on the reservation is aware of who's who among the Medicine Men, or Women, and their reputations sometimes spread far beyond into the neighboring tribes. There are specialists among them in herbs, fractures, bone setting, childbirth, and so forth, as well as rain-makers. The busiest, however, are the diagnosticians. The Indian feels that if he knows the cause of a person's ailment, half of the problem is solved and he can thereby select an expert in that problem. Quackery or insincerity are then ruled out when true knowledge must produce results or be abandoned. If the Medicine Man foresees failure, he announces it before the patient and the audience present, or he recommends someone else with more understanding than he of the problem at hand.

The Medicine Man heals both animals and men by working on the premise that all are rhythms, with different vibratory rates. Are not all the songs which were ever written composed from the same musical scales, only differently arranged? Are not, then, all created things each individual songs created by the Great Song Writer? If some physical or emotional shock has disrupted the life rhythm, it is wisdom to re-establish this through contact with the Great Music Maker who originally created all the individual rhythms.

It becomes clear to us now that the Indian Medicine Man goes far beyond mere hypnosis or the projection of his will upon another. To the Indian, life is a song, an arrangement from the Great Concert Master, who expects man to continue singing in harmony with all the creatures of the earth. For this he developed his gift of theopathy to be used for the harmonious well-being of all the levels of creation.

The Indian believes that eighty percent of all cures must first take place in the mind of the patient, otherwise the physical aids may also fall short. The foundation of a large percentage of the "Miracle Drugs" of modern medicine find their origin in the ingredients of the Medicine Pouch of the Indian Medicine Man who knew and could utilize the herbs and roots so effectively.

Superstition, lack of sanitation facilities, and many other limitations are the by-products of a "civilization" which has robbed the Indian of his former way of life and leaves him ill-equipped to combat the prevalence of modern disease as it now exists. But in the art of restoring the mind of the patient to a "wholeness" where the natural recuperative powers can take over, aside from the medicinal application of herbs, the Indian in his more native state still has no peer.

My first personal introduction to primitive Indian wisdom was at the tender age of four or five years when I accidentally fell backward upon a beautiful specimen of pear cactus! While someone ran for the doctor, the old Indian woman who lived in our household answered my wails by quickly and calmly melting some beeswax in one pot while filling a second with cold water. Dipping me alternately from one into the other, the afflicted area was soon well-covered with a thick warm coat of beeswax which was both soothing and sedative. The final dip into the cold water was long enough for the wax to thoroughly harden into permanent form. With a deft flip of the hand the beeswax was then yanked off, containing each tiny quill intact!

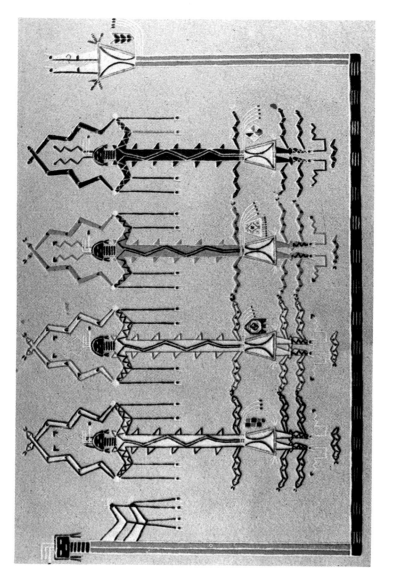

"Wind and Snakes"

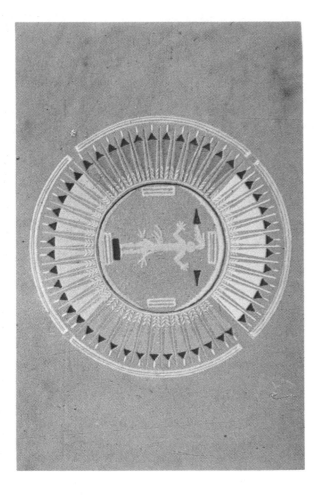

"Sun and Eagle"

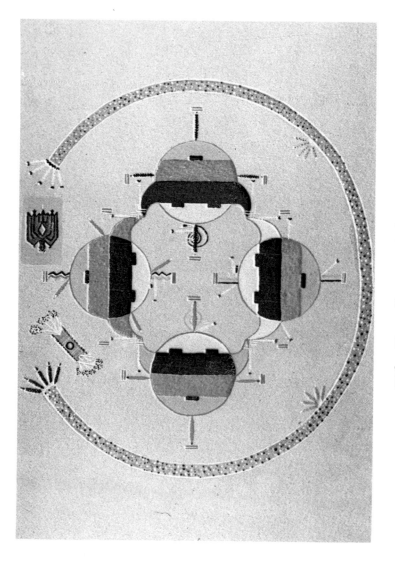

"The Four Houses of the Sun"

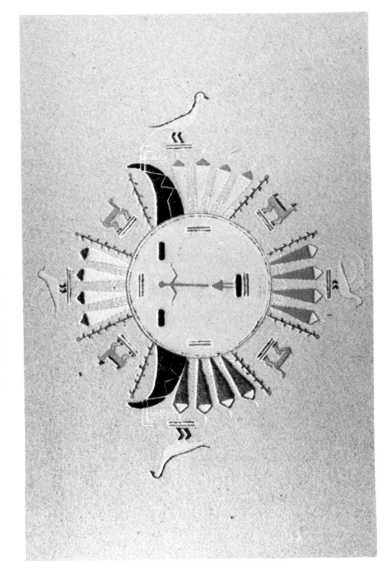

"Chiricahua Sun Sandpainting"

"The Slayer of Alien Gods"

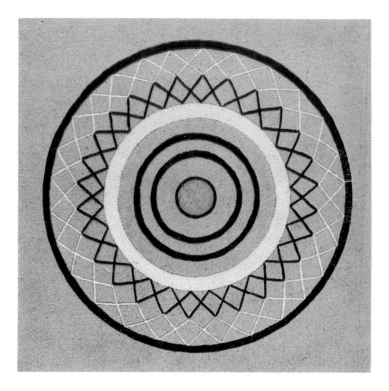

"Southern California Indian Sandpainting" – Funeral

"Navajo Creation Story"

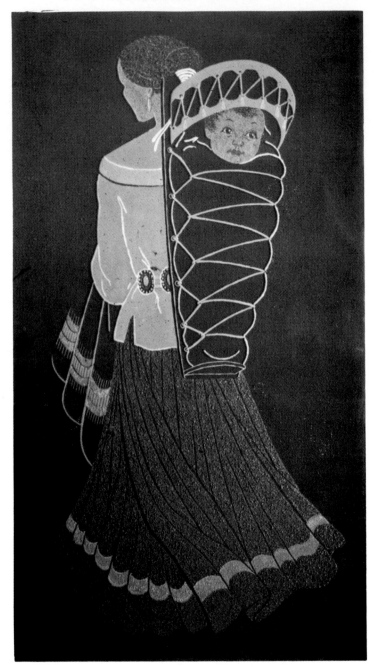

"Indian Motherhood"

The ancient way is the timeless or ever-new way, and the Wise Ones, in tune with the Spirit rhythm and knowledge, know that within the problem itself is usually found the answer on nearly all levels. When there is one in need of healing, or whatever, the event is a blessing, for it carries the divine opportunity for two souls to come together.   In order to do so, there must be a pure desire to help and a pure desire to be helped.   Thus the healer becomes like the light of the sun to the seed, the attraction attracting and causing it to grow with life.   And this mutual fusion, accomplished through the language or rhythm of Spirit (chanting, prayer, and so forth) causes the Catalystic Spark to be present. This the Indian long ago discovered and utilized in his natural environment.

"MESSENGER OF LIGHT"

"Great Messenger of Light,
Bind thy winged sandals
Firm and tight upon thy feet,
And swiftly to thy people go;
And lift the yoke so long worn
In patience, and in silence by thy race.
Give them hope where hope is almost dead.
Kindle in their hearts the fire of love,
And leave dread hatred to hearts less pure.
And thou, oh Messenger of Light,
Have patience to endure.
For thou wilt meet with many trials;
The sages of thy tribe will test thee well;
All may seem dark and thy journey not worthwhile.
Then go into the secret places of thy heart,
And dwell in close communion with the Spirit blest.
I have no fear for thee.
Thou knowest well the tempers of the steel
Entrusted to thy hand.

Oh dawn, receive this messenger to thy heart,
Who from the house of prophets comes.
Receive ye, too, the message he imparts, -
The freedom of thy people to proclaim, -
The first bird's carol in the light of dawn.
Oh dawn, spread the light o'er every mountain peak
And into every dell.
Breath thy morning light into the flower-like purity
Of thy children's hearts;
And dwell in glory of the mid-day sun.
Thy patient waiting is almost at an end.
Thy peaceful watching rewards thee then,
Oh, blessed of the Great Mystery,
Thy time has come. "

    Nipo Strongheart - orator of the Yakima

EARTH - ANIMAL - AND MAN

he Indian's daily life was often conditioned by messages received through observation of the behavior patterns of the little creatures. Most of us have at one time or another observed the geese, or flocks of birds flying south, and sometimes, when the flight is noticeably early, we know that an early winter is in the air. When the swallows return to San Juan Capistrano on the southern coast of California, or when the buzzards return to Hinkley Ridge in Ohio, again we know that spring is arriving for her annual encore in that part of the country.

Mammals, birds, insects, reptiles and even some plants, Indians believe, forecast weather conditions far in advance. The majority of reptiles for instance avoid hard cold winters by burying themselves well below the frost line. It has been said that when the desert tortoise goes into hibernation, it is wise to observe closely how deeply it buries itself. Five to ten inches would indicate a very mild winter; ten to twenty inches, temperate; but if the tortoise goes deeper than thirty-five inches, a hard rigorous winter is to be expected.

Science now can verify some of these remarkable deductions with sensitive instruments. Back in August of 1952 at the time of the Tehachapi earthquake in California, the Indians moved out of the area several days before the impending disaster. The technique used was a simple one for those schooled in the habit of observation. The ground squirrels, chipmunks and all little rodents who lived underground were restless, and refused to return to their burrows even when pursued. It was obvious then that Mother Earth was having great unrest deep within, and, in a few days, the danger would be manifest. Seismologists can now pick up these earth vibrations with some of their super-sensitive instruments, but the little animals, up to now, still have the edge on the scientists. . !

Then there are the forewarnings of the birds, or the little-messengers-of-the-Great Spirit. Should they build their nests on the high, delicate, and relatively unprotected branches, then weather conditions will most likely be mild, presaging light winds and light rains. But should they construct their nests in the rugged, sheltered parts of the tree, then it is almost certain storms are due.

The little one's of the woods winter food supplies also indicate the weather that is to come, as told by the heights at which they store their food along the walls of the arroyos, gullies and river banks. The industrious beaver along the river, stream or lake anticipates high water far in advance and makes preparations for it. The little rodents also, in communion with Mother Earth, will bury their winter's supply of nuts, seeds, acorns, and so forth, low for a moderate season, but, should they seek the higher ground of slopes, hills or banks, then the Indians take note and wisely move their village to higher ground in accordance with the auguries of the little brothers.

Generations of disciplined observation taught the Indian to develop a super-sensitivity to the rhythms of nature and a deep feeling of oneness with all life. In time of danger or in time of need, the Indian called on the spirit and the qualities of the animal to meet the challenge of the changed conditions. For example, when a horse was lost, or game was desired for food, the Indian would prepare himself by going through the rituals of the hunting ceremony and calling upon the spirit of the creature desired to come forth and manifest itself through blending with his own soul in the oneness of the Universal Creative Spirit that made us all. If his heart were pure and his need urgent, this spiritual seeking would often reveal the locality of the one sought and the hunter would go forth humbly grateful and fully conscious of his responsbility for the other's life.

The success of the truly sincere hunter is legendary among the American Indians. Guided by the unseen force, he ofton went directly to his prey, but also he would utter a silent prayer before releasing the fatal arrow, saying: "Forgive me little brother, but I take your life in order to preserve life as I in turn will be taken." But never did he kill more than for his own need, or the need of his people. Even after the animal was killed, he continued the ritual of prayer and chanting that the pure motive of his action might be sealed in the rhythm of life and death and of all creation.

It is well-known that the Indian is a master of outdoor survival. Of the deer, buffalo (who in reality were like a super-market on the hoof), or any other animal slain, 99% would be used. The hair was often carded or woven into cloth; the skin was used for moccasins, buckskin, drum heads, or, if large enough, for ceremonial robes or teepees. The bones became spoons, needles, breast plates, or decorations. The hoofs were made into glue for adhering the feathers to the arrow shafts; the guts were used for bowstrings and for the stitching of bucksin clothing or other leather work. So nothing was wasted from the bounty of the Great Spirit.

THE SOUL OF MAN **

ut of darkness into the light emerged the essence of man searching for his own soul. In some of the Amerindian mythology, the step by step procedure of creation is as follows: First there was a world of total darkness. Light and fire followed. This was the first world. Soon came the down-pouring of torrential rains and the world was completely covered with water. This was the second world - of algae, sponges, fish and all the other marine and water peoples. Then, as the water began to recede, a third world of mud became apparent with the swamp inhabitants: the alligators, turtles, frogs, beavers and so forth. Finally, the fourth world of dry land emerged, and the earth became as it is today, with man being the latecomer. By this time the Great Maker had perfected his technique of obtuse teaching, for simple man's perceptions were not acute. The Indian believes truth has always been, and there exist always Great Souls who know this truth and are Way-showers (usually the Deities or super-natural heroes of their legends).

Man was created from the beginning as man, and each species of animal was directly projected to Mother Earth as a unique reflection of the Great Spirit. Spiritually man was born in darkness, his soul wrapped in his cocoon of ignorance, which would evolve towards the sunlight of self-awareness. A child is like a caterpillar, its adolescence the cocoon stage. Age is not physical, but is a state of mental awareness. Out of the darkness of ignorance a man goes through the purifying fire of pain, trials and tears (water stage). The Indian showed maturity by overcoming tears for pain with a wonderful stoicism and endurance born of training.

The Spirit, says the Indian, is like a universal neutral force, neither positive nor negative, but super-sensitive, available and yielding to appeal, such as that of a Medicine Man. The Spirit, being neutral, can be used by man for man or against man.

The Spirit is a universal essence, the soul an individual expression of this essence. The Spirit cannot get lost; it is nowhere and everywhere. The soul, however, may wander in darkness, unless aware of the guiding light of the Great Spirit.

There is one Spirit, and its reflection in the mineral, vegetable

and animal kingdoms is their spirit, but man's spirit has the ration-
al soul which gives him the responsibility of being the elder brother
of creation. Man needs discipline, however, and the mastery of the
senses to unfold his full potential.   In the heart of man is born the
fruit of love, truth, compassion and justice, thus bringing balance
to the physical world within and around him.   The animal has love,
but it is without reason, and rarely has compassion or justice.   In
a way, a mother's love is symbolic of the Divine Spirit hovering
around the wayward soul immersed in darkness.

It is obvious that the Indian mystics of America knew this
spiritual symbology very well.   This esoteric wisdom is in their
art, but is usually verbally hidden.   There are many reasons for
this secrecy, but foremost the Indian feels that wisdom of the occult
symbology cannot be taught by word alone.   Rather, it is earned
through experience and deeds, observation, meditation and reverent silent contemplation of the realities in every day living.   The
mature soul grapples with the problems of experience and digests
them, giving thanks for the opportunity to excercise the senses as
well as mental faculties, and building strength by conversing with
and understanding the inner self.   When the inner voice of the spirit
speaks, it conveys wisdom to the outer-man if he has the equilibrium of positive silence.   This true knowledge is the beginning of the
mental exercises necessary for the unfoldment of the soul.

There have always been, somewhere or at sometime, among all
the peoples of the world, that rare handful of souls who are the fore-
runners, the great leaders, pioneers and torch bearers in many
fields of the arts, science and religion, and who may or may not
ever have had academic education.   The most spectacular of these
exemplars are the prophets, both the greater and the lesser.
These are the Ones-Who-Walk-In-The-Sky, the Way-Showers.
Some have founded the world's great religions and stand out like
beacons of light, guiding the turbulent sea of humanity. Way-showers all claim to receive the greater portion of their wisdom directly from the divine source, the Great Giver.   Their radiance is part
of the sky of human experience.   These supreme men are the ex-
amples, who, through word and deed, train souls, so that men may
not be careless of the jewels hidden within them, and which are only
in need of discovering and polishing.   Wherever we find remnants
of past civilizations we find evidences of the practice and knowledge
of the laws of attraction and affinity, fasting and silence, master-
keys to a practical application of life, given by those who were

knowers of the Way. Among the American Indians also is the record of this greater-guidance, while, in their legends, are portrayed
the "deities" and "supernaturals" (the heroes and saints), who reflected the Way, and walked tall among their people.

The Indians respected their men of vision even when these men
predicted the doom of their own culture, which the Wise Ones fore-
saw even before the arrival of the pale-faced invaders.   Thus,
Drinks Water of the Sioux and Sweet Medicine of the Cheyennes
were two Holy Ones of the far past who saw the long night that was
coming to their people.

Nearly all the great Indian Chiefs and Medicine Men had strange
visions, and all were known for their integrity, truthfulness, sincerity and nobility, which made them worthy of leadership.   Chief
Long Bear of the Sioux could read the mind of a man at a glance and
had great power and influence over his people.   Crazy Horse had a
prophetic vision very early in his childhood, which was interpreted
for him by a Sioux Medicine Man in great detail. [11] He was told that
he would recognize the events when they came to pass, and that he
was to become a great warrior Chief after he captured a horse of a
particular color with distinctive markings.   Further, he would also have a personal battle with a renowned warrior.   The child
was told that he would lead his people through many successful battles, but that he would be killed while on a peaceful mission by a
treacherous member of his own tribe.   All this came to pass.

Maman-Ti of the Kiowas, whose name means Sky-Walker, or He-
Who-Sees-Beauty-Beyond-The-Stars, was known also as Do-He-Te,
The Owl Prophet.   The white men never knew him as a prophet, only
as a formidable warrior.   But among the plains Indians he was a
most fabulous Medicine Man who could accurately predict coming
events, and was never found to be wrong, even in the prediction of
the time and place of his own death as well as those of others.

Sequoya of the Cherokee nation became intrigued by the white
man's magic of putting thoughts in "talking leaves" (letters, books
and newspapers).   One fine day he said: "It is not magic. I shall
write the language of the Cherokees. " Everyone laughed, of course,
for he did not even know the English alphabet.   He was scorned by
those who considered him a lazy Indian, for he wandered through
the forest talking out loud, practicing the phonetic sounds of words.
An Indian who talks out loud to himself, they thought, could only be
crazy!

But twelve years later, following a solitary struggle, and many frustrations, he redeemed himself before a hearing of the doubting Cherokee Council, where, within a matter of a few hours,   every single member present was able to read and write the Cherokee language! In less than a year a newspaper was being written; poetry, public law, and books were being translated into the Cherokee language, including the Christian Bible. Every child in America should know the monumental accomplishment of this Indian "giant. "   Sequoya, without knowing how to even read or write, invented a syllabic written vocabulary that can be learned by any child in a matter of a few days.   This is truly one of the most remarkable feats ever performed by a single individual, an unheard of accomplishment in all previous history. Most alphabets have been evolved after generations of trial and error.   This feat is a great example of the latent capacities of a kindled soul.

Sacajawea of the Shoshone Tribe is probably the most outstanding Indian woman on record in North America. It was she, a woman of great attributes of spirit, courage, intelligence, endurance and fortitude, who was the guiding light for the Lewis and Clark Expedition in 1804.   Every member of the expedition adored her, greatly admiring her knowledge of the Indian ways of survival, and her shining spirit and womanliness. Both Captains Lewis and Clark, in their documented report to Congress on the Northwest Expedition, gave full credit to Sacajawea for saving their party.

In his farewell oration in 1854 to the white conquerors, the great Chieftain, Seattle, for whom the city of Seattle, Washington, is named, said:

". . . Youth is impulsive. When our young men grow angry at some real or imaginary wrong, and disfigure their faces with black paint, their hearts also are disfigured and turn black, and then they are often cruel and relentless and know no bounds, and old men are unable to restrain them. . ."

". . . We have everything to lose and nothing to gain. . ."

". . . Our religion is the tradition of our ancestors – the dreams of our old men, given to them in the solemn hours of the night by the Great Spirit, and the visions of our Sachems, and written in the hearts of our people. . ."   ". . . And when the last Red Man shall have perished from the earth and his memory among the white men shall have become a myth, these shores will swarm with the invisible dead of my tribe; and when your children's children shall

think themselves alone in the fields, the store, the shop, upon the highways, or in the silence of the pathless woods, they will not be alone. In all the earth there is no place dedicated to solitude. . ."
". . . The white man will never be alone. Let him be just and deal kindly with my people, for the dead are not powerless." - - "Dead did I say? There is no death, only a change of worlds. . !"

From "Chief Seattle's Unanswered Challenge," by John M. Rich. Published by Lowman and Hanford Company, Seattle.

*   *   *   *   *   *   *   *   *   *

Chief Joseph of the Nez Perce Tribe was a military genius, and an expert on guerrilla warfare. His tactical maneuvering was con-sidered a masterpiece of the science of war, worthy of the finest West Point instructors. What the West Pointers never knew is that Chief Joseph was a deeply spiritual man and would never have gone on the war path except for the most intense provocation. He knew from the beginning that his few Indian warriors could not win a war against the white soldiers, and told his younger chiefs why, but the hot blood of youth boils quickly! His wish was to hold his people to-gether, and, like a father, he was there for the sad ending to give them courage to go on living. All the attributes of his noble char-acter were attuned for peace and construction, not for the disin-tegrating forces of war.

Cochise of the Chiricahua Apaches clearly saw the destiny of his own people, the many battles and fights, and even the great wars of the world. "Everything that lives fights," he said, "today we lose, tomorrow you fight, you lose to other people. We all walk the same path of life, until we all learn to live in peace, like brothers and children of the same Earth Mother. Calamities will be with us as usual, as long as men do not learn to love one another as brothers, and become children from the same family."

The Indian parent, particularly the mother, provided the spirit-ual stimulus, as well as the physical pattern of behavior from the time of conception, for the new soul tends to follow the path of the parent. It is imperative, therefore, that a child's parents walk the Path of Beauty, for the young soul is pliable and easily impressed.

The mineral, the vegetable, and the animal kingdoms are all subject to the law of change. Nothing in life ever remains the same but is always in motion, ever changing. Man's progress is depen-dent upon whether he follows his divine nature forward, or slides

backward by following his lower instincts.   Through his lower nature, man expresses untruth, ignorance, cruelty, and injustice,
and by it has perpetrated all the ills of mankind.   Only through a
spiritual awareness of the Creator, and an understanding of the nobility for which man was created can he ever move forward, for
"the source of all learning is the knowledge of God. "

The North American Indians, as a whole, were ascending in
culture and spirit at the time of the coming of the white man to the
American shores.   No other people have been more bountifully endowed, more noble of character and virtue, or more spiritually
aware.   No other people have been subjected to more rigorous tests,
adversities, trials and humiliations, and yet retained the kernel of
their heritage to pass on to future generations.   They have been
robbed of their homelands, their way of life, their self-respect,
and, in many cases, of their pride, and human dignity.

And, yet. . . a man's body may be broken, his will crushed, his
heart sick, but the soul is indestructable.   Should the light of hope,
or illumination from the Greater-Source be shed upon it, like the
phoenix bird of ancient mythology, it can rise again from the ashes
undaunted.

Every human being that lives may reach deep within the culture
of his own background and, with pride and honor, bring forth bed-
rock building stones that will contribute the foundation for bridging
into a better future.

Although past cultures must always give way to change, our
original Americans may stand tall, and, with reverence in their
hearts, pick up the challenge of their ancestors (and despite the
moral decadence about us, which includes all peoples in our present society) help again to show the way through a new moral and
spiritual standard, as echoed by the words of Abdul-Baha:

"Lift up your hearts above the present and look with eyes of faith
into the future!   Today the seed is sown, the grain falls upon the
earth, but behold the day will come when it shall rise a glorious tree
and the branches thereof shall be laden with fruit.   Rejoice and be
glad that this day has dawned.   Try to realize its power, for it is
indeed wonderful!   God has crowned you with honor and in your
hearts has He set a radiant star; verily the light thereof shall
brighten the whole world! "*

*"The Reality of Man, " by Baha'u'llah and Abdul Baha.

SPORTSMANSHIP - WAR - DEATH

n the blanket days the youth of the tribe were given the opportunity to expend some of the excessive energy in rigorous exercise, by competing in achievements. These were not so much with each other as they were acts of endurance and in games that would have the tendency to bring out the very best in the individual. The goal was to improve one's self, to better the record of yesterday, to add cubits to the strength and character, to acquire nobility in relations with friends and neighbors. In sports, where the opportunity was given to everyone to take a chance, even the losers were winners if they were good at losing. Anyone with a strong and healthy physical body could win, but it took a mature, balanced and noble mind to lose gracefully.

The youth of today compete with each other, with other schools, and neighboring towns. With the right motive this is as it should be. In the tribal days of old, warfare was regarded as an opportunity for the young men to demonstrate their skill, daring and horsemanship, but seldom were many killed or wounded. To steal horses from an enemy tribe was not considered dishonorable, nor was confiscating property as the spoils of war, but out-and-out plunder was rare. Stealing was practically unknown among Indians. The act in itself was a disgrace and was severely punished, sometimes by simply banishing the offender from the tribe, or by complete social ostracism. [6]

Among Indians it is a great honor and privilege to lay down one's life in battle, defending the rights and principles of a just and noble cause. When at war the acts of valor were greatly admired and rewarded, if they were achieved without treachery, and preferably without death-dealing. For example, a brave would surprise everyone by dashing into the midst of the enemy, exposing his life and touching with a feather, or a coup stick, an enemy warrior, preferably a chief. This act was very demoralizing to the enemy; it was worse than death. Symbolically it meant many things, but mainly : "I could have killed you with my war club, but now you live on because I was trained well by my people and their medicine is very good and strong." Sitting Bull gave a performance like this when he was only twelve years of age. His act was credited with winning an important battle for his people when the enemy exposed themselves recklessly, trying to even the insult.

In most tribes it was considered the sacred duty of an Indian brave to mourn the departed soul of anyone killed in battle, whether it be of his own war party, or that of the enemy. He would steam-bathe inside a small hut made of willows stretched with buffalo skin, using water sprinkled over hot stones to make steam. He would paint his face, then fast and pray for the period of a moon (month) before resuming normal relations with his family.

Each Indian had a "Death Song" which he sang only in time of battle or when exposed to great danger. All members of the war-ring party were expected to take part in the purifying ceremony afterward whether or not they were personally responsbile for taking life. It was expected of them to seek forgiveness, and to pray for the safe journey of the departed soul(s) through the spirit world's lands of mystery and the long long sleep, to the path of the rainbow colors, insuring a safe return to the Great Beyond. The departed enemy would have done the same for him had the circumstances been reversed.

Suicide was considered an unreconcilable act, for, to consciously take one's own life was to invite disaster for the soul. One does not enter another's house uninvited. When one commits suicide he is, without question, renouncing this world, and he has not been invited back to the home of the Great Spirit. He, therefore, belongs to neither, and becomes a soul lost in darkness, condemned by his own hand.

On the other hand, joy and laughter were considered akin to prayer as great releasers of tensions, both creating a constructively balancing force for body and mind. The Koshare, Mudheads, and other clowns, who form a part of the various southwest Indian ceremonials, are given a position of importance as they teach the people to laugh at themselves objectively, and help prevent any person from taking himself too seriously. Seek the joy of being alive, says the Indian, for the final reward is the return of the body to Mother Earth and the spirit to Father Sky.

DEATH AND DREAMS
(The Long Long Sleep)

eath, the Indian believes, is as great a miracle as life, with the soul's condition in the hereafter dependent upon what we have made of our lives upon the earth plane, even as our physical lives are conditioned by the womb. Our recognition while in the physical realm of the greater metamorphosis that comes with death is little more than our understanding while still in the womb of what the new life will be like when we are born.   In both cases our faculties or knowledge are not yet developed enough to grasp the nature of the as-yet unreached realms of being that lie ahead of us.

The cocoon is the tomb of the caterpillar from which the butterfly emerges, but how much more wonderful is the free flying life of the adult insect as compared to the worm-like and quiescent stages that preceded the time of glory! Man's life is like the caterpillar stage, and death's beginning is the cocoon stage, while the soul is the butterfly that survives the long long sleep, freed from all the limitations of physical existence.

For the Indian death is closely related to sleep, for, in sleep, he may recognize flashes of the past, premonitions of the future, and experience the fourth dimension in which both time and distance are telescoped, and, in the flicker of an eyelid, can transcend both time and space.   Thus sleep is the stage where the physical mind has a chance to become acquainted with the subconscious or the reflection of the soul during the state of slumber, and also experience some of the freedom from limitations that will come after the long long sleep.

Dreams thus serve to train the mind by pre-conditioning it to accept future coming events in the land of the great beyond.   Dreams are like a barometer, or a map, which may indicate our physical progress, or lack of it on this earthly plane, in relation to our spiritual unfoldment.

When a person has a repeated dream sequence, a nightmare, fantasy, wishful pattern, or whatever, it should be viewed as an inner revelation, a subconscious self-analysis, prompting the conscious mind to become aware of the hidden thought patterns of the daylight hours. Dreams are guidepost signs that could be studied carefully, for, like finger prints, they are unique and tailored to the individual. Dreams among the Indian people serve to explain the "inner man" to the "outer self, " or the conscious thinking mind in relation to the "spirit self that dwells among the stars" (the soul, or the superconscious).

The Indians believe the soul is aware of the best course for its own unfoldment even though it is a servant to the free will and the choices that it makes during the sojourn on earth. This is why even the most evil of men sometimes have flashes in which they wish heartily, for the moment at least, that they had chosen to lead honorable lives. Our five senses are the weakest as well as the strongest links between the physical and spiritual spheres of action, depending on whether the will is directing the energy of the body in harmony with the cohesive element of the Universe, which has been called by various names: - Wakonda, Great Spirit, Massau, God, Great Mystery, Creative Force, and so on.

The severe physical training of the body and the senses that is characteristic of most of the old Indian life stemmed partly from the Indian's deep religious belief that the body is the temple of the living spirit, and must therefore be strong and disciplined to reflect this perfection. Prostitution or perversion of one's own body or that of another would be to make a prison of self, resulting eventually in a moral decay far worse than physical death.

The Indian feels the senses and their training are most important. In modern terminology, the five senses may be referred to as the feelers or antennas. The mind is the transmitter and receiving set, and the heart the transformer with its unlimited power for love, or hate, to broadcast, receive or shut off through the will. The Indian feels very strongly that, as long as you have the mastership of the senses, you can extend these inner feelings beyond the mountains to see what is going on. While modern scientists have done just this with the telephone, radar, radio and television, the Indian feels that a far greater and more beneficial power of vision and thought extension lies within each of us. He says that the white man thinks with his head (intellect), while the Indian thinks with his heart, and, for this reason alone, he is more closely related to the mineral, the vegetable and the animal kingdoms, for each responds more readily to the loving rhythm of the heart. All of the Divine Teachers have taught that the spiritual heart is the seat of the inner mysteries of the Great Spirit.

The Indian believes in the continuity without interruption of waking and sleeping hours to such a degree that, during the Initiation or ceremonial rites the Medicine Man or Woman observes closely the sleep patterns of the individual, hoping that a prophetic dream or vision will come through the initiate. Often the Medicine Man will say, "We saw the Bird spirit (or bear, or snake, or raven, and so forth) upon your face. Each of these symbols have a special meaning to each particular tribe. Among the Paiutes, for example, when one dreams of the flight of the falcon, it symbolizes an adventure like scouting or hunting. Different animals have varying symbolic meanings also, as does the coyote with his quality of great cunning. How to explain each dream correctly, whether wish-fulfillment or genuine prophetic vision, is the task of the Medicine Man, even as modern man, in his society, turns to the psychoanalyst.

Scientists concede that the physical body, the senses, the mental patterns and the emotions have a tremendous influence and bearing on our subconscious thought patterns. The balance or imbalance of these processes are revealed in our dreams. For example, if one is not meeting his problems in conscious life adequately and a tension is building up, the subconscious often takes over in his dreams and either answers these problems or pinpoints the need for them to be answered before a nervous breakdown or other dangerous personality problems. Answers may often be revealed in the dream pattern.

The Indian believes this too, though he may explain it differently. What modern psychologists have discovered about dreams is what the Indian has always had in his feeling about his sleep life. Man is like a bird with two wings that potentially can lift him to the pathway-of-the-stars (spiritual life). Too often, however, he is like a bird with a broken wing. One wing is the physical conscious thinking process, and the other is the spiritual, including the subconscious dream pattern. When both wings are functioning with the rhythm of the Beauty Path (Spirit Path), they have mighty power, and can carry the soul to joyful heights.

The term Beauty Path is a complete spiritual concept covering the soul experiences and forming a way of life. Death could be a "heavenly dream" or an "eternal nightmare" depending not only on how one has lived his life, but also upon the state of consciousness at the moment of his passing on to the next world, that is, whether it is spiritual or non-spiritual. For this reason the religious rites, or the Death Chant or Song are considered vitally important when the time of the transition is near, for this is a prayer. Prayer is an integral part of the Indian life and a part of his preparedness for the greater life to follow. It is a conscious attunement with the higher forces, which the Indian well understands, and it is with prayer that he begins and ends each day, and with which he greets the new born babe, or his departure from this earth.

The sum total of all his life deeds, actions and thoughts while in the physical form, destines the soul's path in the next world of experience. His character - capacity for and the use of love, compassion, integrity, bravery, honesty, or the reverse qualities, is like an identification card which must undergo the stamp of the divine IBM machine, which selects the particular vibration for the next plane of action. Whatever this pattern be, it is the one which the conscious mind has earned and unconsciously selected for his soul (or faltered, by failing to select), and in which it is therefore to be born anew.

The rhythm of the night and the rhythm of the day are obviously different. To the American Indian the spectacular drama of the dawn and the sunset, each with their streaming clouds of glory, when dark and light change guard, has a definite effect on his physical, mental and spiritual attitude. His personal life, as well as that of his tribe, is in tune with the infinite when he prays with ceremony at the dawn and again at nightfall. Strongly aided by the prophetic dreams and visions of the Wise Old Ones, his religion and belief in life both here and hereafter, as well as his personal life, are all paralleled by the rhythms of the day and night and of the seasons. Daytime symbolizes physical life for the conscious mind and body, and night time symbolizes sleep and death of the conscious mind. Here the vital activity of the unconsious, or the dream pattern, is given freedom. This mysterious spirit of the soul of the individual is the real life and the real self, which is no longer under the restrictions and limitations of the physical body.

The dramatic march of the seasons also play their important role in the Indian's pattern of life. The resurrection of all life comes with the springtime; the return of the Spirit of the Giver of Light, and the rebirth of the morning sun, sunrise.

Summertime parallels the mid-morning sun, which is like the young man, ever boastful, the green and aggressive warrior, the young adventurer flexing his strong muscles of productivity, until he arrives at the zenith of the high noon sun of maturity.

And the fall, or autumnal equinox, symbolizes the day's middling age, when man begins to reap his bounty of wisdom.   The seeds of character that he planted in the early springtime of adventurous youth have reached the ripe stage of abundance or fruition by the afternoon of his life, or harvest time.

Wintertime, preface to a slumbering earth, and sunset, prelude to the night, proclaim the time of transition to the long, long sleep. When man is old enough to have the wisdom to release the mind and the soul to the freedom beyond the sunset on the pathway of the stars, he goes in peace and beauty like a moth that has been swept by its love of light into the flame of the fire and disappears in a flash of glory.   Mother Earth receives him and the shortcomings of the physical body are no more, but the soul ascends to a higher realm unrestricted by its previous limitations.

The Indian mystic, we can thus see, feels an obligatory and sacred duty to pray at sunrise (symbolic of new life), and at sunset (the end of light and the beginning of the Great Mystery), so that physically, mentally and spiritually he is in rapport with all creation at any given time of the day or night.   In life he is as he will be in "death," and hence will be welcome at the Great Council in the World of the Great Beyond.

The names of the dead are never spoken for they have returned to the home of the Grand Father Spirit, and no one must use their sacred names in vain.   The fire that is the Center of Being has flamed up and welcomed home its own.

*   *   *   *   *   *   *   *

(Body and Soul)   + – TWIN SELF – +   (Sky and Earth)

My Twin has gone beyond the horizon,
And I have gone deep within Mother Earth.
My Twin has become the twinkle of the star,
And I, (flesh and bones) food for the underworld.
My Twin is the guiding light for the weary traveler,
And I, the fragrance of the blossom, the flavor of the corn.
My Twin inspires the Beauty in you,
And I make your body healthy and strong.
My Twin and I have journeyed through this world before,
And will return again in One body, One soul, One Spirit.

SOUTHERN CALIFORNIAN INDIAN SANDPAINTING

(Funeral Ceremony of the Luiseño Indians; see page 78)

f the two styles of sandpainting that occur among the Southern California Indian peoples, only the Luiseño sandpainting seems to have survived. It is mostly concerned with funerary ritual, depicted in simple, abstract designs and done with two colors, utilizing primarily white ashes and coal dust, plus the natural color of the background. Both the ashes and the coal dust are symbolic of the fire, or life that has gone out of existence, and returned again to the place of emergence. The center of the painting represents the "Navel of the Universe" or the psychic umbilical cord that connects Mother Earth with all her children, symbolic also of our utter dependence upon the earth for physical survival.

Once an old Indian woman of 110 years said to me: "When I go on the long sleep I would like my body placed in the earth wrapped only in a blanket, that it may feed my little brothers and create a new civilization in the underworld. They have served me well these many years helping to produce the many good things to eat."

The worms, bugs and scavengers, such as the polar bear in the far north, wolves and buzzards, who are assigned to the task of decomposition of bodies, are recognized by the Indians as essential in maintaining the balance of nature and thereby helping to sustain the vegetable and animal kingdoms in the eternally evolving life cycle.

"All pass through the process of composition and decomposition – a natural law to which all are subject. This law is ruling throughout creation and forms a bond of connection among all created things." *

This law the Indian accepts and gives thanks for the portion allotted to him in the one great scheme of creation.

*Quoted from "The Promulgation of Universal Peace," by Abdul Baha.

NAVAJO CREATION STORY

(Navajo Coming Up Story; Life Way Chant; see page 79)

 rom the Great Central Spirit (central circle) four torches reach out to illuminate the four quarters of the world. A white bar going from east to west and ending in yellow crosses, is intersected by the yellow bar going from south to north, and ending in white crosses. These crosses represent three rays of light, or the twelve Golden Rays or laws by which an Indian guides his life. The white represents the essence and purity of the spirit of light, while the yellow indicates a state of initiation. The black-dressed figure lying asleep next to the round hogan is the Celestial Fire Keeper Hashjehjin - a godlike spirit who first thought out the mystery of fire and deposited or hid it in the wood to challenge man's mind, and to develop his ingenuity and resourcefulness. The criss-crossing on his shoulders and arms is the Milky Way. The fire stick that he is holding in his right hand is the selfsame one first used in producing fire by friction. In his left hand he is holding a medicinal charm ring, and a powerful medicine pouch that contains all the sacred rituals applicable to all the diverse uses of the Magic Fire Ceremony.

From the fire symbol below the medicine pouch (black cross) a red trail line is left by Coyote who stole a burning torch from the fire circle of the sleeping Fire Keeper, and, in the process of doing so, burned his claws. After a long, arduous journey throughout the four quarters of the sky, Coyote finally delivered the stolen fire to Earth's First Man (round head) and First Woman (square head), sitting near the round black hogan, with the fire symbol at the doorway.

Coyote is highly respected by the Indians, for he is the personification of the spirit of the Hunter-Warrior. Coyote has the most remarkable recuperating powers. He seems to come back from the dead after being mortally wounded to prove once more his remarkable ability to survive. He steals things continuously, but avoids capture and the traps set for him. In desolate desert lands he finds food if there is any to be found, thus preventing starvation. (The stealing of food when one is hungry is not frowned upon by Indians, for food is free to all, even if there is none to offer it.)

Among the Navajo (Dineh-the-people), it is said that the cunning of the Indian warrior who knows where he is and where he is going, even in darkness, is like the homing instinct of animals, due to the guiding Spirit of Coyote. -- For centuries both the native peoples and modern man have been guided through the darkness by the "Coyote or Wolf Spirit" (or the "Little Bear Spirit"), which is the name given by the Navajo to Ursa Minor and the north star (or the constellation of the Little Dipper).

You will notice in this sandpainting that Coyote avoided crossing the House of the Sun and the Eagle, but during his entire journey favored traveling under the cover of darkness by way of the house of the Moon. There was also a glow of light from the Rainbow Guardian beneath his feet to guide and protect his long and perilous journey throughout the Houses of the Sun, the Moon, the Stars and the Constellations before arriving at his final destination, the hogan of the First Man and First Woman.

*   *   *   *   *   *   *   *

When the Indian wise men are asked about their ideas on the origin of man, one hears several intriguing versions and theories on the evolution of man in North America.

There are many legends of how the ancient people journeyed down from the north across the sea of ice, over mountains and rivers.

The Aztecs of Mexico have a legendary history covering over three hundred years of traveling southward from the northern part of the American continent, although they cannot trace their beginnings farther north than what is now the southern part of Colorado and Utah or near the area where the Pueblo Indians of Arizona and New Mexico are located today.

This is not so, however, with some of the Pueblo Indians, particularly the Hopi of Arizona. Their story relates that for thousands of years they have been in the same location and are an original group belonging to the dark race. Man was created as man, they say, and certain of their ceremonials bear witness to the mythological time of this first emergence into the "fourth world" or earth.

According to Hopi belief, as well as others, there is only one race, the human race, which is divided into two major groups: dark and light (like night and day). Further subdivision yields the four races, belonging to and bridging the rhythm of the day and the rhythm of the night. (Similar to sunrise, noon, sunset and midnight, or the four seasons: spring, summer, autumn and winter). To the dark-skinned peoples were given the gift of perception, the gift of knowing. To the light-skinned peoples were given the gift of recording and the gift of doing.

Through his prophets the Indian knew of the coming of the white men, with faces-like-the-dawn, from across the wide waters, and welcomed him. Even knowing that his own culture, as it were, would eventually give way, the wise Indian accepted the greater truth, that only when the two peoples come together at the center and share their gifts would each receive a Greater Gift than either alone can ever know.

In some of the Indian legends it is said that after the Great Destruction and when the water had receded there were many lands and the people were no longer there. They had been swallowed by the Great Flood, and there was no trace of them anywhere.

When the land became dry the ancient Hopi Indians were instructed to go to the four quarters of the world as emissaries of good will and to tell people to remember always to be grateful to the Great Creator and to be kind and good, and not to make war upon one another. If they did not obey there would come out of the sky a gourd of hot ashes so terrible that when it fell upon the earth it would destroy everything within a great area of land where no grass would grow for many years.

The first group went east, the second group went south, the third group went west, and the fourth group north. They had to cross a sea of ice. The Hopis scattered all over the earth, during which time they have changed the color of their skin many times. How then can one be identified as Hopi? A Hopi is A Peaceful One; anyone on the face of the earth who worships the way of peace, the brotherhood of man, and keeps the Commandments of the Great Spirit.

MOTHERHOOD

(See color plate on page 80)

any animals have the ability to blend into nature for safety, and this the Indian developed also to a marked degree. Silence was their first requirement for survival, for the slightest sound could give the family away to the enemy. To this end the prospective mother meditated in solitude, which is invested with the perfect equilibrium. [6]
Hers was a path of true devotion, of prayerful recognition daily of the Unseen, the Mysterious, the Eternal.

In some tribes, when a baby was due, the mother would go all by herself, and, within a few days, return with her precious little bundle. When the baby was born, instead of the slap to start him breathing, the mother would place her loving lips upon the baby's mouth and impart the "Breath of Life." The arrival of a new soul upon this earth should be a loving, tender experience, with only the most sweet and gentle of memories associated with this miracle of birth. . . instead of the shock (spank) that often initiates one's beginning into our "civilized world."

If the baby should start crying or making other noises, it could be dangerous, especially if the mother or the family were hiding from an enemy. To prevent the baby's crying the mother would gently clamp the nose of the baby, closing off the air supply momentarily, while at the same time singing softly, something like this: "Hush, hush. . . my precious one, my little one. . . listen to the Voice of the Spirit, listen. . . listen. . . how it . whispers through the leaves around us. . . hush. . . hush. . . let the spirit speak. . . !" The lesson was quickly but gently learned, without loss of security or love.

The coming of a new life to the Earth Mother must always be associated with love, silence and reverence, laughter and joy, for these are the first lessons a new soul must learn, and there is a joy in being alive. The patient devotion of the mother was soon assumed in a prayerful attitude by the child who feels himself a part of all that is - and a kinship with all created things. For there is life in rocks and minerals, as there is life in the mountains, in the forest, in the clouds and in the desert. Everywhere there is life. All things, both the animate and the inanimate, are therefore personified, for is not each indivdual an expression of the life-giving force of the Sun Spirit without which there would be no earth family? Only through the manifestation of Mother Earth in relation to Father Sky, can we know anything of the Great Mystery - the emanating Central Force, whom no one has ever seen... But we hear His voice upon the wind, His joyful rhythm in the morning breeze, in the sweeping majesty of each new dawn; in the re-occurring miracle of life, in the cheerful melody of the birds, the delightful tapping of the rain, and in the frightening thunder of a storm-tossed sky...!

Another lesson each new soul must learn is that of detachment. With this aim in mind, the Indian Mother prepares the cradle board to carry the child on her back, or, on some occasions, hangs the cradle board with the baby from a gently swaying tree branch, where the motion of the wind will be associated with that of mother's walking rhythm. The baby is usually placed facing towards the family group, where the "Rock-a-Bye-Baby on the Tree-top" would be part of the relationship of the wind, the birds, the tree, the fire, and the home.

The Indian Mother, knowing that she is but the vehicle through which the new soul manifests, faces her child away from her where he may become acquainted with his Maker, while yet feeling the nearness, the rhythm and the love of Mother.

Wind, sand, silence, and sunlight are the earliest playmates of the Indian child, who soon comes to know that each individual creation of the Great Spirit has its own special purpose, and each brings its own priceless gift. From the Flower People, the Butterfly People, and the Spider People, we learn of beauty, color and harmony; while the Bird People come to teach us of Music - of freedom and joy, as they sing the Song of Life.

And the Indian Child learns early that, in reality, the whole Cosmos is but one great family, and we ALL are the children of the ONE GREAT SPIRIT...!

PREDICTIONS - SIGNS OF OUR TIMES

 ractically all the holy books of the world have predictions or prophecies. The Hindu, Hebrew, Zoroastrian, Buddhist, Christian, Islamic and Baha'i writings, all contain rich literature of things past, present and yet to come.

Among the North American Indians there was no written form, but there is a vast amount of history, mythology, traditional rituals and predictions committed to the depth and breadth of their memories, aided by the symbolic designs of their arts and crafts, and ancient records in pictograph on cave and canyon walls.

Every Indian tribe has at least one Medicine Man or Woman with the ancient wisdom to advise, counsel and often to prophesy. Several of these glimpses into the future, which I heard from the Wise Old Ones about thirty years ago, are worthy to note:

"Great happiness (Peace) will be coming to all the peoples of the earth, when the Indian Spirit returns in other skins to the Americans." (The white race of all the people of the earth have been the most smugly unaware of this Spirit.)

"The Ancient 'Breath of Life' will be recognized again by the white Medicine Men." This prediction has been fulfilled so far only in part. A few years ago (1957-1958) the Life Guard Association adopted the resolution that breathing directly into a drowning person's mouth was the best way to bring him back to life.

Now obstetricians are beginning to have prospective mother's have their babies the old Indian way, with the body inclining or in an upright position. Some day, perhaps, the good doctors will recommend that the mother should place her loving lips on the baby's mouth and give the "Breath of Life" to her own child. . . !

"The more the white man advances in iron knowledge (technical), the more he has to adapt to the ancient ways of our people."

The jet pilots, going through the desert survival training, eating insects, weeds, snakes, cactus and so forth, have learned this. . So have army men in the jungles and sailors shipwrecked on strange shores.

While the following statement is not a prophecy, it is a tale of partial retribution. In 1828 the United States Congress passed the Indian Removal Act. The white man had discovered gold in the land of the Cherokee Nation! Laws were passed to justify annexing and confiscating Indian lands and placing all Indians of the area in what were essentially concentration camps. But these were friendly Indians that had fought on the side of the Union against the French and the English, and many of whom were now prosperous contributing farmers and artisans. Thanks to the genius of Sequoya, they even had their own newspaper written in their own language!

Cherokees, Choctaws, Chickasaws, Creeks, and Seminoles - 14, 000 souls in all - were driven like cattle through rain, snow, and summer heat. More than 4, 000 died on the way, leaving a path of graves extending from the Blue Ridge Mountains of Virginia to the Oklahoma Territory, known as "The Trail of Tears." This truly black chapter of brutality, only lightly referred to in American History, was reenacted in a lesser scale upon our own American soldiers during the "Death March of Bataan." In the former the U.S. Army was the oppressor, while in the latter it was the oppressed.

In their new lands west of the Mississippi the Indians set about rebuilding their lives and their homes through hard work, knowing that in time all things would be balanced. It is paradoxical that the Indians were pushed onto the most unwanted and desolate lands, generally for their reservations. Yet, as technology developed and oil was needed, it was discovered in the Oklahoma wastelands of the Cherokee Nation. Oil and uranium were found on the Navajo Reservation and a secret ingredient of the fuel for rockets and satellites comes out of Death Valley, which was formerly Paiute territory.

There were many prophets among the Crow Indians who predicted the coming of the white men, the disappearance of the buffalo, and the coming of the "spotted buffalo" (cattle), the "fire-boat" (steamboat), the "iron-horse" (train), "wagons-in-the-air" (airplanes),etc. These and other predictions have been well-documented by Frank B. Linderman in his book, published in 1930, entitled PLENTY COUPS, and reprinted in 1962 by the University of Nebraska Press.

"It is good for man to have his head in the clouds, and let his thoughts dwell among the eagles, but he must remember also that the higher the tree grows into the sky, the deeper the roots must penetrate into the heart of Mother Earth."

The Indian wise men realized that their society had achieved a moral, ethical and spiritual balance in most cases, but they knew also of the coming of the East People who would emerge from the wide waters across the path of the sun and bring a great change to their way of life.   But the Old Ones predicted:

"These people-with-the-faces-of-the-early-dawn will bring great knowledge, strange and foreign. " Also they said:

"All strangers are potentially gods in disguise; honor them as such until they prove that they are not. "

The white strangers brought thunder sticks (guns), and great grandfather thunder (cannon), and beasts (horses) on which they rode as swiftly as the wind.   They were truly like deities, for they used thunder and lightning with reckless abandon.   The Conquistadores, though warmly welcomed, soon fell off their pedestals as gods.   Their cruel behaviour, murder and plunder, proved beyond doubt that they were false gods, as were many of those who came later, and pushed their way across the continent.

The centuries have come and gone, but not their dreams.   Now, more than ever, our wonderful advancing technological science and and civilization is like a one-winged bird.   How can it fly without the balancing wing of the Spirit?   Pure, unadulterated, unattached, the selfless Spirit that has no bondage, or name, but is like unto music, its rhythm understood by all through the universal language of the pure in heart.   Do not all races, all creeds, want this Path of Beauty?

The Indian had risen to a height of moral and spiritual development rarely rivaled.   The material civilization which has taken the place of this original American culture is now rocketing to dizzying heights of technological and material development, with our finest minds channeling their energies toward greater weapons of destruction, jet-propelling the world to a threatened total extinction, unless we can re-establish a balance with the spiritual forces.   When the material world can recognize, accept, and combine its mental greatness with the spiritual dynamic which is the heritage of this American continent through our predecessors, only then can we hope to balance the two wings of the bird, and soar to far loftier heights than either culture alone could ever accomplish!

*   *   *   *   *   *   *   *   *

Some strange Hopi prophecies.

The following story has taken about thirty years for every frag-
ment of the jigsaw puzzle to fall into place, for each part has been
delivered at a different time and place by events not seemingly con-
nected with each other, but, like the warp of a tapestry, all has finally developed into a meaningful design.

In the summer of 1931, while on a long visit to the Hopi Indian
Reservation and the Monument Valley Region in Arizona, I had the
opportunity of hearing many wonderful stories. Many were as yet
unknown to outsiders, so we were told by our venerable old Indian
guide, and had been passed from father to son for thousands of
years. For some peculiar reason, he had selected our group of
strangers to give an intimate glimpse into the life of his people.
Perhaps he was aware that some one in our group had a definite part
in the pattern of dreams that, at times, foretell significant events to
come.

With three old cars in our caravan and no roads or maps, we
were continuously in need of native help. Divine providence had
provided this Indian guide for us. Fortunately our friend spoke
Spanish, like many of the elders of his generation, some of whom
were related through marriage with Spaniards or Mexicans.

"Yes," he said, "we were told many years before the coming
of the strange white people that the Great-Giver-of-Life would sometime send to our mesas men with the true Spirit-of-Beauty in their
hearts. They would have as symbols, the Spirit of Peace and true
Brotherhood that will unite all the children of the Earth. This Spirit will begin to return when mistrust and wars will be among men
and between earth and sky."

"Earth and sky?" someone interrupted.

"Yes," he said, "the face of Father Sky will be criss-crossed
with smoke (cotton trails) and fire-wagons-that-fly-in-the-sky.
This will be at the time-of-the-end when our ways and our culture
will be no more, and a ribbon-like rock (paved highway) will follow
the path of the sun from sunrise to sunset across our pueblos and
mesas. Strange fire-wagons (cars) will move upon them with the
swiftness of the antelope running away from danger."

It was strange to hear this story in 1931 when even trails were
not often apparent on this vast reservation, and even my home town
of Tucson, Arizona, had barely any pavement. In fact, only major

streets had pavement up to the edge of town. The city of Phoenix was the same, and highways were only gravel roads at the time. It is possible, of course, that some of these predictions had been adapted from other tribes, as I have noticed in some cases, but truth is still stranger than fiction, the reality greater than the prophecy!

Subsequent years and other visits to the Hopi country showed the story unfolding into truth. There was a sudden rude awakening when uranium, gas, and oil, were discovered in both Navajo- and Hopi-lands. Paved highways became ribbons-like-rock stabbing through the virgin landscape from sunrise to sunset, with the exception of a thirty mile stretch from the Hopi mesas towards Tuba City.

For years there were rumors that the Hopi leaders were trying to hold back progress and the fulfillment of an old prophecy. As long as the ribbon-like-rock was not completed, they could keep their traditions and their way of life intact; but, when the road was completed, it would mark the time-of-the-end. They would lose their culture and a strange new way of life would invade their homeland. It was further predicted that seven years from this date would mark the time of the "Great Purification Day." This they feared more than anything else, for, unless all men learned to live together in peace, they felt all would be destroyed.

When, after many years of postponements and delaying tactics, the last section of highway was completed in 1957, a ribbon-like-rock had become a true fulfillment of the ancient prophecy. The next logical step was unavoidable. The Hopi Spiritual leaders must journey towards the sunrise where the land meets the wide waters (sea). Here it had been said there would be a large meeting house where the "sun-shines-through-walls." They had been told from ages past that one day all the big chiefs from the four quarters of the earth would meet here in council.

Six spiritual leaders of the Hopi Indian Nation and their interpreter, Mr. Thomas Banyaca, a member of the Sun Lodge of Hotevilla Mesa, arrived in New York City at the great "glass house" of the United Nations. They requested an audience, but were told that it required three months on the agenda before they would have an opportunity to be heard. At the Pentagon in Washington, D. C., they were confronted again with red tape and protocol. Fortunately for the record, some alert reporters became interested in the human element involved, resulting in the ancient message and warning of of the Indians receiving wide publicity on both the air and in the press.

The warning to all the peoples of the earth was given to the Hopi People by Massau, the Great Spirit, following the Great Flood of the long-ago-time. The warning was this: All men must be like the Hopi People, peaceful and as brothers to mankind throughout the four corners of the earth ("Blessed are the Peace Makers"). They must never make war upon each other or a "gourd of ashes" would fall from the sky and wherever these ashes touched all would be burned and the grass would not grow for many springs (H-bomb and fallout). There was no alternative to this message; either all men learn to live together in peace like our Hopi brothers or all would be destroyed. (Hopi means "The Peaceful Ones".)

"We shall wait for three sunsets," the Hopis informed the reporters, "and then shall return to our villages. We have done as we were told to do long ago. All those that have ears to hear must follow the peaceful way of life to true brotherhood!"

Some of the Hopis themselves began to have doubts regarding the effectiveness of this trip or the meaning of the prophecies when time passed and nothing seemed to happen. Only a few small religious groups here and there paid attention, and these sincere ones invited the Hopis to share their lodging.

One Hopi, Thomas Banyaca, remembered these doubts as foretold by his wise old grandfather, who had said to him in that long-ago time that on a future day when he most greatly questioned the Hopi prophecies he would see "people jumping from hilltop to hilltop." After this experience, according to his grandfather, he would know with a certainty the wisdom of the ancient ones, and the dark clouds of his doubts would disappear.

So it was that on the very morning of his deepest soul-searching and prayers regarding the message of his people, he was in a hotel room in Denver, Colorado, when he looked out the window to suddenly see a man "jumping from roof top to roof top over the buildings!" It was on this particular morning that the U.S. Army Ordinance Department was demonstrating for the first time publicly its new rocket-propelled "flying belt" to be worn by the individual combat soldier of the near future to avoid the canyons and other obstacles of a difficult terrain.

In strange ways indeed are the prophecies of the Old and Wise Ones demonstrated to their doubting children!

TAPESTRIES IN SAND

 n 1931, at the age of sixteen, I accepted the job of "chief cook and bottle washer," to pay for my share of the expenses as a member of a group of artists from the University of Arizona and the Tucson Art Institute who were making a several months sketching tour in the northern Arizona desert country.

Early one morning, while encamped near Kayenta, I took off alone with sketch pad in hand, to the top of a nearby mountain. The incredible panoramic majesty of the valley below was breathtaking. Agathla Peak, which I later learned was one of the holy spots of Navajoland, thrust from the flat desert floor like a staggering monolithic monument to an Atlas race. My very soul seemed lost in the sheer magnitude of the beauty before me. An intermittant attempt at sketching brought an acute awareness of the frustrating inability to capture the grandeur of Monument Valley on a mere piece of paper, and a realization of the pathetic futility of attempting to express the overwhelming tide of emotions surging within me. How can one attempt to contain the ocean in the puny thimble of self. . ? I wondered at the silken patch of soft red sand on which I sat, carried there probably by the singing desert wind from the shifting red dunes far in the valley below. These were no ordinary sands which slipped through my fingers like a soft caress on that windswept mountain top of excelsior experience!

I felt that something of me would stay there forever, that something of this magic would be with me always, - and, even though the afternoon shadows had lengthened indicating that I must go, yet I could not. I was seemingly gripped by an invisible force, producing quivering hands which would not subside. Impulsively, unconsciously, I gathered handfulls of the soft red sand and filled my pockets. Only then was I at rest to descend to the distant camping grounds and resume my chores.

The following day I attended my first "sing" and watched a Navajo Medicine Man create an unbelievably beautiful sandpainting. For days, weeks, and months afterwards, ground, sandstone, and symbols were an integral part of my daily life. The unquenchable desire to know, to do, to learn was ever present and soon I was teaching others how to make sandpaintings upon the ground.

Many years later my wife and I decided to cross the Navajo Reservation through the Goosenecks of the San Juan River, Mexican Hat and Kayenta to the Grand Canyon. We were advised not to attempt the dirt and gravel roads following the heavy rains (paved highways came later), but the magnetic attraction was too strong. As the irresistible current sucked us south towards Navajoland, I was enveloped with the exuberance and expectancy of the homing instinct, which has no apparent purpose save the obeying of an inner command.

At a bend in the road of the throbbing red earth and the intense blue skies of Dineh-the-People, I impulsively stopped the car, for there before us were the magnificent red sand dunes of long ago. It was like dipping my quivering hands into an ocean of recollections as they sank into the soothing silken sands. Again the pull was too strong to leave until two large paper bags from the back of our car had been filled with this unbelievably beautiful texture.

One late afternoon, weeks after returning to our California home where I was teaching arts and crafts to children, I was beset with the problem of what to do with the excess adhesive plastic which I had mixed for class. It was a versatile new development, but one which could not be saved once the catalyst had been added. Already I had filled all the cracks and crannies of our workshop, and stood holding the container, sorrowful that I knew no further diversified use for this fine material. Suddenly my hands began to quiver with quick uncontrollable movements. Momentarily this inexpressible experience left me without recall. Then there flashed the vision of desert road and the silken red sand. I was seized with the feeling of extraordinary discovery! Sand? Sand and plastic? Quickly I combined the two, and my first successful Tapestry in Sand was born.

It is amazing how these strangely beautiful and mysterious forces of the spirit weave an intricate rhythmic pattern around and about us. Seemingly there is no connection between the mountain top, a sand dune at the bend of a lonely desert road, and a humble work shop in the city. . . . all nourishing the same unconscious childhood dream at the root of the silent subconscious, until the reality of it blossoms before the unbelieving eyes. What glorious seeds are planted within us. When? And by whom? Only in humble and grateful silence can we hope for the mystery to be revealed through the language of the soul.

ACKNOWLEDGMENTS

Many have touched my heart with help and encouragement throughout the long period of research and struggle in assembling the first sandpainting exhibitions and subsequent development of this book, but to a few I would like to give special acknowledgment: Miss Leila Livingston Morse (grandaughter of Samuel F. B. Morse), who was personally responsible for my first one-man show of Navajo Ceremonial Sandpaintings at the Museum of Natural History in New York City; the late Dr. Gladys A. Reichard of Columbia University, who gave permission to reproduce some of her original research from "Navajo Medicine Man;" Miss Mary C. Wheelright of the Navajo Museum of Ceremonial Art in Santa Fe, New Mexico; Dr. F. W. Hodge of the Southwest Museum in Los Angeles, California; Mr. Robert Ariss of the Los Angeles County Museum, for his unfailing encouragement; Mr. Nipo T. Strongheart of the Yakima Indian Nation for the inspiration of his wisdom; Mrs. Tatzumbie du Pea (115 year old Paiute Indian) who adopted my wife and me as her children; Mrs. Dawn Edwards Polprasid, without who's insistance (and assistance) "Tapestries" would never have been written; my wonderful wife Jean for her invaluable aid in the correcting, rewriting and editing; Vinson Brown, who believed in its worth for publication; and to Miss Helen Richardson, who's faith and interest helped sponsor it.

SUGGESTED REFERENCES

1. Abdul Baha. The Reality of Man. Baha'i.
2. Alexander, Hartley Burr. World's Rim, Great Mysteries of the North American Indians. 1953, Univ. of Nebraska Press.
3. Arnold, Elliott. Blood Brother (Broken Arrow). 1950, Meredith.
4. Brown, Joseph E., editor. Sacred Pipe; Black-Elk's Account of the Seven Rites of the Oglala Sioux. 1953, Univ. of Oklahoma Press.
5. Collier, John. Indians of the Americas. Norton.
6. Eastman, Charles Alexander (Ohiyesa). The Soul of the Indian. 1911, Houghton Mifflin.
7. Forrest, Williams. Trail of Tears.
8. La Farge, Oliver. American Indian. 1960, Golden Press.
9. Reichard, Gladys A. Navajo Religion, a Study in Symbolism, 2nd Edition. 1963, Pantheon.
10. Rich, John M. Chief Seattles's Unanswered Challenge. Lowman and Hanford.
11. Sandoz, Mari. Crazy Horse, The Strange Man of the Oglala Sioux. 1962, University of Nebraska Press.
12. Seton, Ernest Thompson. Gospel of the Redman. Seton.
13. Wheelright, Mary C. Navajo Creation Myth.
14. Willoya, William and Vinson Brown. Warriors of the Rainbow, Strange and Prophetic Dreams of the Indian Peoples. 1962, Naturegraph Publishers.

15. Wyman, Leland C. Navajo Indian Sandpainting: Symbolism, Artistry and Psychology. 1960, Taylor Museum.
16. Hodge, Frederick W. Handbook of American Indians North of Mexico. 2 volumes, boxed. Rowman.